GROWING STRONG

Women in Agriculture

November 1987

CANADIAN ADVISORY COUNCIL ON THE STATUS OF WOMEN

Graphic Design
Grauerholz and Delson, Montreal

Cover Photo
Jean Glover of Waterford by
Vincenzo Pietropaolo

© Vincenzo Pietropaolo

Prepared for the
Canadian Advisory Council on the
Status of Women
Box 1541, Station B
Ottawa, Ontario
K1P 5R5

Available free of charge from the
Canadian Advisory Council on the
Status of Women

Catalogue No. LW31-25/1987E
ISBN 0-662-15202-6

Cette publication est aussi disponible en
français.

This publication is dedicated to
the memory of Rosa Becker, in the
hope that recognition of the work
of women in agriculture will
become a collective concern.*

PREFACE

Women play a major role in the Canadian agricultural sector but, until now, their contributions have been largely ignored. The work women did on a farm was usually viewed as the natural continuation of the role allocated to them in the home.

The Council is therefore proud to present this new book *Growing Strong: Women in Agriculture* which describes not only the conditions and roles of women working in agriculture, but the challenges they face in their attempts to become visible, in the family, in the community, in a national context.

It is important that all Canadians recognize the realities of farm women today and assure them the full legal, social and economic status they deserve. It is also essential that the voices of farm women in Canada are taken into consideration when designing programs and policies to address their varied needs. The CACSW is confident that *Growing Strong* will be invaluable to the public, parliamentarians, and to those involved in the agricultural industry in Canada.

Sylvia Gold
President

TABLE OF CONTENTS

ACKNOWLEDGEMENTS 5

This publication would never have been possible without the cooperation and support of many individuals. I would like to mention some of these people, and thank all those whose names I was unable to include here.

My thanks to Monique Bernard, a member of the CACSW, and to Dianne Harkin, a former member, both of whom are farmers by profession; my thanks as well to the many women farmers' groups that since 1985 have provided suggestions concerning the content and direction of this study and have allowed me to use the results of their work and experience. I would also like to acknowledge: the help of Marie Burge, Philip Ehrensaft, and Ray Bollman, who provided basic statistics and information on the contribution of women to maintenance of the family farm; the assistance of many participants in the second Conference of Women in Agriculture, held in Prince Edward Island in November 1985; and the many suggestions from Marion Meredith, Patricia J. Storey, Liz Delahay, Suzanne Dion, Fran Shaver, Elaine Driver, Barbara Humenny, and Lorraine Garneau.

Finally, I would like to thank the authors for the wonderful spirit of teamwork that developed among us. My gratitude goes as well to the CACSW staff who helped at various stages in the production of this publication.

Diane Morissette
Research Co-ordinator

INTRODUCTION

by Diane Morissette

The Canadian Advisory Council on the Status of Women (CACSW) chose to focus this publication on women working in agriculture not because of the numbers they represent (two per cent of the Canadian population), but because of their vital contribution to running the family farm and to Canadian agriculture as an economic activity.

The agricultural sector and the agri-food industry employ nearly 1.45 million Canadians, and generate almost ten per cent of the gross domestic production,[1] through activities as diverse as food transport, processing, and packaging, as well as the sale of fuel, agricultural machinery, fertilizers, and other materials. These figures show that agriculture is in no way marginal, but is a vital component of our economy. Consequently, it is important to be aware of the conditions under which a great deal of our food is produced; as well, the position that women hold in the social organization of the family farm or in the emerging non-family agri-business must be clarified.

By publishing this document, the CACSW is fulfilling its mandate, which is to report to both the general public and the federal government on the living conditions of Canadian women, and on their diverse contributions to the development of this country.

At present, the role of women in agriculture is still unclear in many respects. Throughout history, and almost everywhere on earth, the gathering, processing, and preparation of food within the domestic sphere have been activities carried out primarily by women. But in North America and elsewhere, agricultural work in its myriad forms is usually viewed as the natural continuation of the role allocated to women in the home.

Women farmers' groups in Canada have worked very hard to redefine the economic nature of their work, which is all too often taken for granted. Yet most of Canada's agricultural production comes from independent family business, which in 1980 accounted for 73 per cent of all agricultural products sold.[2] Therefore, the time that women spend working on the farm directly benefits all consumers.

Although the CACSW does not want to speak for the women farmers who have made their concerns known these past years, it does hope that this publication will better document the conditions and role of women working in agriculture, and will put their claims in a national context.

Because this document is intended for several audiences, it is in the form of a collection of articles. With this one publication, the CACSW hopes to direct the attention of city dwellers, decision-makers, those responsible for programs to promote the economic health of Canadian agriculture, and women farmers themselves to a number of topics.

The first article of this publication describes how the collective needs of Canadian women are also central to the concerns of women who live on farms. These concerns include access to child care and to services for women who are victims of violence, the adoption of measures promoting health and safety on farms, and access to training programs that take into account the many roles that women farmers play. Ginette Busque also focusses on the cost to society of ignoring such needs. She ends her article by presenting a number of initiatives that have been introduced in various areas of Canada to meet these needs.

The second article reports on progress during the past ten years toward recognition of women as agricultural producers and partners on the family farm and toward recognition of the consequences for women farmers of their lack of formal status within the farm business. Michelle Boivin also describes what marriage and partnership law can offer in the way of such status. This recognition is essential so that each member of the family who works on the farm can play an active part in making decisions and running the business, and can, at the very least, be taken into consideration in Canadian agricultural policy. A number of changes are necessary to reach these goals, namely a shift in attitudes and in mentality, a reform of our banking and legal institutions, and a new approach to considering the joint endeavours of husband and wife. These are preconditions for equitable recognition of the hours and the energy that women devote to agriculture.

The third article briefly reviews national statistical data and uses on-the-spot interviews to describe the characteristics and working conditions of the itinerant agricultural labour force, which is made up mostly of immigrant women. Julie Lee's article is an important contribution, given the lack of public debate on this little-known and overlooked group of agricultural workers.

The fourth article of this publication provides an in-depth analysis of unpublished data from the agricultural census and the 1981 general census that pertain to the economic contribution of women to agriculture. In addition to the demographic aspects of women in agriculture, Pamela Smith also indicates the proportion and number of hours that women farmers work on the farm itself, or off the farm at a paid job, depending on the different ways they contribute to the operation. This section also shows that a large part of food production depends on free labour, especially the free labour of farmers' wives, and that very few of these wives benefit from legal recognition within the business. In 1981, eighty-seven per cent of family farms still belonged to a single owner, usually the husband.

Many women farmers' groups have presented these facts during the past ten years, but undoubtedly this is the first time that the census data have been analysed in terms of the economic and legal non-recognition of women farmers' work. Politicians who look to statistics for a profile of Canada's work force will find in this analysis a useful model to interpret these data, but will also realize that such statistics have their limitations. At a time when governments are being pressured from all sides to take into account the unpaid work of women when calculating gross national product or gross domestic production, Pamela Smith's article indicates approaches that could be useful in this regard.[3] The author also provides an overview of statistical trends related to the participation of women in organizations that promote farming interests, and in agriculture-related training at colleges and universities.

I hope that, after reading these articles, parallels between the situation of female agricultural producers in Canada and that of women farmers in developing countries will be evident. The objectives of the 1985 Nairobi Conference, which marked the end of the United Nations Decade for Women, were to pool experience and to demonstrate the truly inter-ethnic and international nature of the women's movement. Issues such as access to credit, access to property, agricultural methods that respect the environment and the quality of life of farm producers, the involvement of women in measures to develop the long-term viability of agriculture, and technology adapted to its users emerged as mutual concerns for women farmers from both halves of the globe.[4] In Africa, women grow eighty per cent of the food crop.[5] North America presents a different reality, in which the contribution of women farmers falls within the framework of a partnership between wife and husband on the family farm. Yet this difference in no way negates the similarities between North American and Third-World women farmers, in that there still is a long way to go before all the women farm producers around the world obtain complete social, legal, and economic recognition of the crucial work they do.

I also hope that reading these articles will help in tempering the preconceptions that city and country people in Canada hold about each other. Market rules have led us to expect an adversarial relationship between consumers, who want lower food prices, and the people who produce the food. Our grocery shelves are fully stocked, but what compromises have to be made by women farmers to achieve this for us?

Above all, the CACSW hopes that women farmers' groups will be able to use material from this publication to speed up the institutional changes necessary to break Canadian agriculture out of its male-oriented mould.

1. G. Walford and P. Lys, "Value-added: Agriculture's Impact on Other Industries," *Agrologist*, vol. 14, no. 2 (1985).

2. Data taken from: Canadian Advisory Council on the Status of Women, *Women in Agriculture*, fact sheet (Ottawa: November 1985).

3. Paragraph 120 of the Nairobi Forward-looking Strategies for the Advancement of Women, adopted in July 1985 at the World Conference to Review and Appraise the Achievements of the United Nations Decade for Women, is very explicit:

   The remunerated and, in particular, the unremunerated contributions of women to all aspects and sectors of development should be recognized, and appropriate efforts should be made to measure and reflect these contributions in national accounts and economic statistics and in the gross national product. Concrete steps should be taken to quantify the unremunerated contribution of women to agriculture, food production, reproduction and household activities.

4. Environmental Liaison Centre, *Women and the Environmental Crisis*, a report on the proceedings of the workshops on Women, Environment and Development (Nairobi, Kenya: July 1985).

5. Debbie Taylor, "Women and Analysis," in *Women: a World Report: a New International List Book* (London: Oxford University Press, 1985), pp. 16-28.

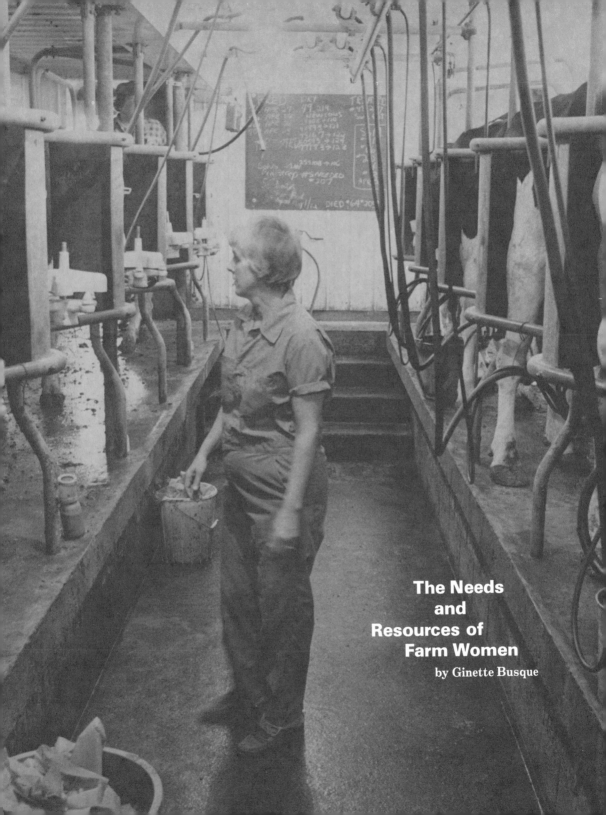

The Needs and Resources of Farm Women

by Ginette Busque

1 TABLE OF CONTENTS

ACKNOWLEDGEMENTS

This study was made possible by information gathered by the author during telephone interviews with farm women or people involved in agriculture. From Newfoundland to British Columbia, the people contacted generously agreed to give their time to answer questions. It was felt that the interest they showed in this study was a guarantee of its relevance. Use was also made of documentation published in recent years on the subjects discussed in this article. Although the material currently available is of great interest, it is incomplete and thus does not allow as detailed a picture of the situation as the author would have liked to present. Further research and data collection are essential.

Ginette Busque

Any consideration of the needs and resources of farm women requires consideration of the problems that they face. Such consideration, however, runs the risk of presenting a distorted picture of their real condition. As the farm women interviewed for this study often pointed out, their image, as projected by the media, is clichéd and stereotyped. In order to avoid these problems and to form a clear and accurate picture of farm women's reality, farm women were the chief source of information.

The quality of life for agricultural women is affected by many factors, including child care, health services, violence, and access to training. Farm women are currently demonstrating interest in all of these areas.

Our health follows from our poor quality of life.[1] (*translation*)

In Quebec, it's the women who attach the most importance to questions of quality of life and quality of the family farm . . . It should be remembered that child care is not solely the responsibility of women.[2] (*translation*)

Of course, other needs are just as important, and deserve immediate attention. Access to credit and property, for example, is at the heart of the economic situation of farm women, a situation that is, in turn, at the centre of their status within the farm community. However, in the present article, the concern is with what might be called the *principal needs* related not to the status of farm women, but to their ability to carry out their tasks and to develop as women in a world where their contribution is vital.

The topics examined herein reflect the concerns of farm women highlighted in the few surveys and research projects carried out in Canada on the needs of these women. All those interviewed in the course of this study confirmed the relevance of this approach to studying the needs of farm women.

The world of agriculture is distinct from other sectors of economic and social activity. As far as possible, an attempt was therefore made to outline specific profiles of certain needs in order to derive appropriate solutions. In this article, several solutions are proposed for each need. It was also deemed of interest to bring attention to a number of projects that have been tried in some regions.

The author does not claim to have explored all possible avenues or to have inventoried all initiatives. This was not her aim. The emphasis is on suggesting a few directions that might support or inspire women who want to improve the present situation.

Child care has emerged as a major issue for farm women, regardless of whether they work at paying jobs.[3]

Parenting responsibilities are numerous, and do not change in nature according to the area in which families live. Neighbourhood or district, however, have an important bearing on the ability of parents to cope with their responsibilities and to provide for the needs of their families.

Canadian society has long regarded the tasks of rearing and supervising children as first and foremost, if not to say solely, the responsibility of mothers. Since the care of children, especially preschool-aged children, has been considered an individual responsibility, there has been little examination of the nature and extent of responsibility that the community should assume in this area.

In the case of school-aged children, attitudes have changed somewhat faster, since the community's responsibility to give them access to an educational system is no longer questioned. Child-care services, however, are still inadequate both for school-aged and for preschool-aged children.

Nevertheless, attitudes do change. The situation of contemporary women is creating new challenges and new needs. Women in the farming sector are no exception to these changes. As Pamela Smith points out in her article included in this publication, more and more farm women, like their sisters in the cities, are taking on employment outside the farm, and devoting more time to that employment. At the same time, farm women continue to have slightly more children than do women in urban areas, although the gap is diminishing.

Thus, like women in urban areas, women in farming areas are being compelled to remain in or to rejoin the labour force in order to provide financial support to the family or the family business.[4] In some cases, paid employment off the farm is simply a way for young couples to acquire the money necessary to take up full-time farm work.[5] But most often, the salary earned outside permits maintenance of the farming operation itself.

According to data already presented in this book, farm women* spend about 40 hours a week on farm work.[6] Occupational tasks are often combined with family responsibilities. One Ontario study reports that 53 per cent of mothers with children under 12 years of age bring them to the fields while doing farm work.[7] In light of this, the issue of the safety of farm children becomes critical. The danger to children in the workplace is one kind of stress; leaving them alone at home is another.

A large number of farm women, whether working in the fields or carrying out administrative duties, face the problem of access to child-care services. Many of these women also participate in community activities or attend meetings of farm women or women's groups. The need for child-care arrangements that are adapted to a variety of circumstances is therefore evident.

Canadian statistics show that in rural areas (there are no specific statistics for the farming sector), as in urban areas, parents make most use of informal child-care services, either in their own homes or in the homes of a caregiver. It seems, however, that fewer children from rural areas than from urban areas are placed in child-care centres, probably because of the absence of such centres in rural areas. Kindergartens and nursery schools are equally used by rural and urban families. (See Table 1).

It is clear that more farm women would entrust their children to the care of other persons during working hours if this were possible. Preliminary results of a survey conducted in Quebec by the Bureau de la répondante à la condition féminine (BRCF) of the ministère de l'Agriculture, des Pêcheries et de l'Alimentation du Québec, through the agency of the newspaper *La Terre de chez nous*, indicate that 100 per cent of the women with children aged 0 to 17 months said that they needed a child-care service; 96 per cent of those with children from 18 months to 5 years expressed the same need. This corroborates the findings of another study, conducted in Saskatchewan, of 1,708 families with children under 13 years of age. Women in farming areas were no different from those in urban areas in their desire for child-care services.[8] The National Farmers' Union and other groups, such as the Association des femmes collabora-

* In this chapter, the term "farm woman" is used without reference to the woman's status in the farming operation. It designates, in a broad fashion, a woman who works in agriculture.

trices and the Quebec Provincial Committee of Farm Women, have also expressed urgent child-care needs in rural areas by submitting briefs to the Special Committee on Child Care.[9]

Studies and reports on the situation of farm women reveal the need for services — especially child care — enabling them to fulfil their parental obligations. In Ontario and Manitoba, dissatisfaction with provision of child care[10] and lack of available child-care centres during periods of peak farm operation[11] as well as during job training and retraining periods has been expressed.[12]

Information received in the present study strongly supports the studies and reports cited above. Increasingly, farm women have become concerned for the safety of their children and, to varying degrees, have expressed the need for support in fulfilling their parenting responsibilities.

The eagerly awaited report of the federal Task Force on Child Care (distinct from the Special Committee on Child Care), which was made public in March 1986, is not very explicit as to trends in farming areas. However, it does mention that most studies on child care focus on urban areas, and it insists that "a significant proportion" of women in rural regions doing farm-related work give a higher priority to work in the home than to other kinds of work on the farm, and that their husbands are frequently available to provide child care. These observations suggest a trend toward return to a traditional way of life, a trend also mentioned by several women interviewed for this article. However, they totally ignore the increased number of women working outside the home. Be that as it may, the report nonetheless states that:

> . . . both urban and rural mothers who worked full-time indicated a marked preference for licensed care for all ages of children needing care.

> . . . more than 40 per cent of both urban and rural part-time working mothers preferred nursery school/centre care for preschool-aged children.

> When these findings are matched with preferred care arrangements, they suggest that a large proportion of both urban and rural families were not using preferred arrangements.[13]

The Solutions

Becoming aware of needs is certainly the first key step to take, but equipping oneself with useful tools for action is more complex. Farm

Table 1 : Number of preschool-aged children (0-5 years), by rural or urban area

	Canada	Maritimes	Quebec	Ontario	Prairies	B.C.
Rural	729,351	131,617	192,579	162,008	168,200	75,032
Urban	1,442,351	100,676	397,454	560,655	217,262	166,304

Preschool-aged children not in the exclusive care of their parents

In Rural Areas	Canada	Maritimes	Quebec	Ontario	Prairies	B.C.
Total	334,037	46,725	81,127	93,903	73,223	39,059
	45.80%	35.50%	42.13%	57.96%	43.53%	52.05%
Kindergartens/nursery schools	146,400	17,617	33,119	43,099	33,035	19,530
	43.82%	37.70%	40.82%	45.90%	45.11%	50.00%
Child-care centres	14,293	2,585	2,831	4,447	2,708	1,722
	4.27%	5.53%	3.48%	4.73%	3.69%	4.40%
In the parents' home	118,275	18,608	35,831	26,379	23,711	13,746
	35.40%	39.82%	44.16%	28.09%	32.38%	35.19%
In another person's home	128,187	15,972	21,267	44,156	33,854	12,937
	38.37%	34.18%	26.21%	47.02%	46.23%	33.12%

In Urban Areas	Canada	Maritimes	Quebec	Ontario	Prairies	B.C.
Total	799,157	45,405	223,496	312,017	118,148	100,091
	55.40%	45.10%	56.23%	55.65%	54.38%	60.18%
Kindergartens/nursery schools	337,211	15,777	67,490	147,170	57,721	49,054
	42.19%	34.74%	30.20%	47.17%	48.85%	49.01%
Child-care centres	113,084	5,582	37,131	36,371	19,706	14,295
	14.15%	12.29%	16.61%	11.66%	16.68%	14.28%
In the parents' home	286,622	19,823	87,360	95,089	34,505	49,845
	35.86%	43.66%	34.09%	30.47%	29.20%	49.80%
In another person's home	277,080	12,624	80,502	121,333	41,155	21,467
	34.67%	27.80%	36.02%	38.88%	34.83%	21.45%

Source: Canada, Statistics Canada, "Survey of Child Care, Child File – Ottawa," Ottawa, 1981.

work is not comparable to other occupational sectors, and therefore requires tailor-made solutions.

Judith Martin, of the Canadian Day Care Advocacy Association, maintains that, "as much as possible, rural people should be assisted NOT to think of day care as it exists in urban areas. But to think of the kind of support that rural families could benefit from."[14]

In order to devise services that will be of benefit to farm women, it is essential to take into account factors differentiating their needs from those of the majority of urban working women, that is, work at all hours of the day and night, peak periods, a high degree of geographic isolation, lack of public transportation, etc. The social isolation of children in small families should also be considered. These factors, together with the farm women's need for child care, clearly demonstrate the necessity to adopt flexible and diversified arrangements. Ideally, these arrangements should include child-care co-operatives, drop-in centres, all-day centres, and temporary services. There is also demand for child care in the parents' home, a solution generally less-favoured in urban areas. In the rural survey conducted in Quebec in February 1985 by the BRCF, this child-care arrangement (in the parents' home) was the first choice of 46.4 per cent of the respondents.[15] Rebecca Sugarman reports that the majority of traditional farming families in Wellington County, Ontario, also preferred home care, at the same time recognizing that this arrangement has its shortcomings: the difficulty in gauging the quality of the care dispensed, and the risk that the child may not be stimulated and socialized.[16] In the study referred to by Sugarman, the parents rated care in the home of another person as their second choice, provided it was no more than approximately 15 kilometres away.[17]

Because household work and farm work are often closely connected, access to child-care services should not be seen as the only possible solution to the difficulty of farm women in reconciling their various roles. Domestic help would be extremely useful at times, and could be considered as staff in the service of the farming enterprise, since many tasks done in the home, such as preparation of meals for hired workers, are of benefit to the farm.

Initiatives

In Wotton, Quebec, an experimental project, accepted by the Office des services de garde à l'enfance du Québec, was initiated at the request of farm women. The second trial phase of this project ended in August 1986.

The Wotton project differed from the usual family child-care services offered by accredited agencies, in that parents could choose between placing their children in the caregiver's home and receiving, in their own homes, a caregiver recognized by the Office des services de garde. The parents were required to sign a contract with the caregiver; the home of either party had to satisfy health and safety standards of the Office des services de garde. The arrangement guaranteed one day of care per week; the work done by the parents during the care period had to be farm work. Twenty places were available through this project which ended in 1986.

Wotton also offered family child care supervised by an agency, which was the kind of arrangement usually approved by the Office. In this case, caregivers received the children in their homes. This service was intended for rural children in general, and not solely for farm children, although a certain number of places were reserved for the latter. This agency accommodated 50 children, and was responsible for the experimental project described above.

In the region of Waterloo, Ontario, plans have been made to ensure better care for the many children entrusted to unstructured services or cared for in the parent's home. Caregivers would thus have access, through the regional child-care centre, to a toy bank, child-care workshops, information on child development, and a register of local child-care services. Workshops on health, first aid, and home safety would also be part of the program.[18]

A study by Women for the Survival of Agriculture reports that the Ontario government has invested one million dollars to set up and run "16 new rural child care centers, two experimental centers . . . and to provide more subsidized spaces in rural areas." Thirty more rural centres, accommodating 1,000 persons, were scheduled to open their doors in 1985-1986.[19] Although fragmentary, recent data from the Ontario Ministry of Community and Social Services tend to confirm this statement, at least to some extent. With regard to child care, there appears to have been a marked rise in the number of subsidized places and an increase in grants for low-income parents during the period in question. Further, it is estimated that there were more than 100 documentation and information centres in rural areas during this period.

Finally, four rural pilot projects have been set up to evaluate various child-care needs. However, it is not yet possible to determine the exact amount of money and resources allocated to each project, or to make distinctions between rural and urban areas.

Also in Ontario, the Wellington Rural Network for Child Care is of particular interest. The goal of this project, launched jointly by the Ministry of Community and Social Services and the University of Guelph, is to provide support for existing services in order to ensure the flexibility necessary to satisfy rural child-care needs. The network took part in a survey of the need for child-care centres and offered coordination and information services in such areas as toy loans and speech therapy. It also played a role in developing the Erin Child Care Outreach and the North Wellington Child Care Resource Centre programs.

Erin Child Care Outreach is a type of rural resource centre specializing in child care, providing a data register of persons offering child-care services. It organizes activities involving the community, such as workshops and seminars on child care and education. The 1985 *INFO ERIN DIRECTORY* contains a great deal of information on activities for youngsters and services available in the region. The Toytown Library lends toys to children and serves as a drop-in child-care centre.[20]

The North Wellington Child Care Resource Centre also offers (or is planning to offer) programs and activities suited to the needs expressed in the region. Among other things, a register of child-care services is made available to mothers; those who use it have the chance to enjoy some time to themselves. The centre also supplies home care training and offers a program for teenaged mothers.[21]

In Prince Edward Island,

> . . . a successful mobile resource called Play and Learn (PAL) has been operating since 1982 under a National Welfare Grant from Health and Welfare Canada. This program, which operates out of Montague serving nine communities in King's County, offers opportunities for parents and children to come together to learn new skills, to play, to seek support and to interact in an informal environment.[22]

In Manitoba, almost half of family child-care spaces are offered in the rural areas of Interlake and Westman. Training sessions for caregivers have been given in community colleges in Red River, Assiniboine, and Keewatin.

Other projects may be under way elsewhere in Canada. An index of

these does not exist, and the present study was not intended as an exhaustive survey.

In all of these current or proposed projects, the question of cost is of major concern to farm women. Too often faced with problems related to the economic survival of the farms themselves, they have little or no money left for child care. There is no question that women's equal participation in all phases of public life is restricted by the lack of child-care support services.[23]

Therefore, achieving equality for women should be a major rationale for demanding child-care services and other services related to care and education of children and teenagers.

From this perspective, the author fully supports the recommendation of the Report of the Task Force on Child Care, that:

> ... the federal government initiate the development of a nation-wide system of child care in Canada, by declaring its willingness to share a substantial portion of the cost of such a system, and initiating a new federal-provincial cost-sharing arrangement for child care.[24]

> Country living is healthy living? Forget it.
>
> Marie Potvin, grower (*translation*)[25]

City dwellers, deceived by the image of the rural population created by the media, imagine that farm dwellers are protected from sickness, and are strong, vigorous, healthy, and independent. The truth is that working in agriculture is no protection against illness; in fact, farm work itself generates health disorders and injuries. Maintaining quality of life in the farming sector is closely linked to the degree to which health is promoted through social and health services.

The women questioned about health-services needs of farm women expressed varying opinions. Those who do not live far from urban centres are quite satisfied with their access to medical services for common sicknesses and health disorders. But those who live in more remote regions are obliged to travel long distances to receive medical treatment.

Even in these cases, however, if the health problems are not acute, or if a means of transportation is available, farm women seem to cope with their situation fairly well.

> Farm women aren't complainers and few are prepared to sing dirges.[26]

It is when the services of specialists are needed, whether in an emergency situation or on a regular basis, that distance from large centres causes greatest dissatisfaction and harm. Studies dealing with the issue of farm women's health services needs report a growing concern about the lack of specialized services.[27] There are fewer doctors per person and fewer hospital spaces available than in urban centres.[28] It is also true that physicians and surgeons are concentrated in a few cities with high population density. These factors create a disparity of health services not only between urban and rural areas but also between the urban areas themselves.[29] One example of the urban-rural disparity can be found in Saskatchewan, where people living in farming areas account for 19 per cent of the total population and for 44 per cent of the rural population, one of the highest proportions in all of the provinces. However, to serve rural Saskatchewan — a population of 405,145 — only one psychiatrist, one pediatrician, and four gynecological obstetricians have been counted.[30]

Obviously, the absence of gynecologists, pediatricians, and services for handicapped children and the elderly is a frequent source of worry for women. In some regions, no information service is available on family planning, and abortion-related services, of course, are even more scarce.[31] One fact remains certain: rural women's judgement of health services is determined by their ability to travel the distances separating them from the centres where those services are available.

Furthermore, farm women face a whole range of problems unique to farm work. Like their husbands, they are at times harmfully affected by the use of insecticides and various chemical products. It is not possible to deal with all health threats to farm women within the context of this study. Therefore, only the phenomena already studied or observed will be discussed.

Use of Chemical Products

A study carried out in New Brunswick on the links between use of chemical products and the rate of abnormal births in that province (which is higher than in other provinces) revealed that the highest abnormal birth rate is found in an area of intense agricultural activity. Variations in the rates of these types of births are linked to the ways the soil is used and to the seasons during which farming is done.[32] The study deplores the limited information available on the agricultural use of chemical products, but its findings are sufficiently conclusive to justify further research, with emphasis on agriculture-related hypotheses.[33]

In addition to congenital malformation, other kinds of reproduction-related problems — such as spontaneous abortions, stillbirths, and premature births[34] — can be attributed to exposure to certain products used in agriculture. As well, women may develop irregular menstrual cycles.[35] Certain agents of infection are also a danger to the reproductive ability of men and women: the reproductive organs of farm workers of both sexes, when in contact with brucellosis bacteria (brucellae), are vulnerable; infertility can result.[36] Use of insecticides may also, of course, have harmful effects not related to reproduction. Some insecticides widely used on fruit trees and other types of produce are quickly absorbed and transported in the blood, and sometimes attack the nervous system.[37]

Other Types of Health Problems in Farm Areas

Obviously, not all health problems that may result from farm work are related to use of chemical products. Other health troubles most frequently reported by farm workers, and which seem to be most bothersome, include allergies, respiratory problems, back pain, and reduced sharpness of hearing.[38]

The Report of the Ontario Task Force on Health and Safety in Agriculture is of great interest to those seeking information on the illnesses caused by the environment and by farm work. Among other things, the report states that dermatological problems can be caused even by seemingly inoffensive plants, and that many infectious diseases can be spread through handling of contaminated products and animal wastes.[39]

One frequently reported respiratory problem is farmer's lung, which results from inhaling mildewed spores released during handling of damp hay or cereals. In extreme cases, this illness can be fatal. Diagnosis is not easy because the symptoms are similar to those of other ailments, such as bronchitis and pneumonia. The Prairie region, the centre of Canada's grain production, seems to be most aware of this problem. Other respiratory problems are common. Apparently 40 to 70 per cent of the people who work in a cereals or hay environment suffer from inflammation of the nasal mucous membrane ("rhinitis").[40]

Reduced hearing, sometimes noted among farm labourers, seems to be a consequence of the mechanization of farm work, which produces high noise levels.

> Normal conversation measures approximately 65 decibels. Noise in excess
> of 120 decibels causes acute pain to the ear.... Continual exposure to noise
> at high decibel levels over a period of time may lead to permanent hearing
> loss.[41]

For example, a loaded tractor produces 100 decibels of sound when running. It is easy to see that regular use of this machinery, without adequate protection, will lead to hearing problems.

Stress

It would seem that stress is at the root of many physical and emotional disorders of farmers. Of course, stress is not unique to the farming sector, but a great many studies and much testimony have reported its rise on farms. This is cause for concern.

Studies conducted to date have illustrated the relationship between stress and the financial situation of farmers.[42] For example, for women working off the farm to supplement farm income, the weight of a double or triple workload is a source of tension. Given the problem of child care and the long work weeks of farm women (up to 100 hours),[43] it is easy to understand how the incessant demands of farm work can be a source of tension, worry, and stress.

In a study submitted to the Learned Societies by Linda Craig, lack of profit and financial difficulties on farms were identified as the two most important stress-creating factors among farm women. In addition, this study points out that a number of socio-demographic factors contributed to increased stress among farm women:

> Those who perceived that they lacked family or community support tended to fall into the increased stress groups. Similarly, those women who felt dissatisfied with the support they received from their spouse tended to fall into the increased stress group as opposed to the decreased stress group. It was found that the larger the household the more likely it was that the women would fall into the increased stress group.[44]

The Report of the Ontario Task Force on Health and Safety in Agriculture does not underestimate the importance of stress among farmers: on the contrary, it has suggested that the number of farm suicides is possibly the best indice of the seriousness of stress on the farm. Between 1979 and 1982, suicides accounted for 34.8 per cent of deaths, classified as "fatal accidents", on farms.[45]

Safety
It is not possible to speak of health in the farming sector without raising the issue of safety. Interviews for this study with women in agriculture confirmed that safety concerns are universal across the country. The number of fatal farm-related accidents makes agriculture one of the most unsafe sectors of the Canadian economy. The Report of the Ontario Task Force on Health and Safety in Agriculture states that fatal accident rates in agriculture are substantially higher than rates in the construction industry, and about the same as those in the mining industry.[46] In the years 1980 and 1981, 143 children were killed on Canadian farms.[47] To these fatal accidents must be added all the other accidents whose victims have been handicapped, temporarily or for life. Complete statistics for these are not available.

Modern technology has only increased accident rates.[48] Farm mechanization, promoted because it increases farm production, has led to use of powerful machines, which facilitate work in the fields and in other sectors of farming activity, but which are also potentially dangerous.

For example, tractors, like much of farm machinery, are built in such a way that they can overturn easily. These vehicles are not designed to carry passengers, even though they may be equipped with protective cabs (Roll-Over Protective Systems — ROPS). As mentioned, many farm women bring their children with them when they work in the fields. In its September 1985 issue, *Farm Women News* asked its readers to try out child seats in tractors equipped with cabs.

> We wanted to know if it's possible — or if it will **ever** be possible — to transport children safely while working in the field.[49]

The conclusion of this test is unequivocal: for the moment, it is absolutely unsafe to take children along in tractors as passengers, whether or not they are placed in child seats or even in infant carriers or back-packs strapped to the operator. And this was the opinion of all the experts consulted. Furthermore, the presence of children is an additional source of stress, which in turn increases the risk of accident.

Other types of accidents occur on farms. For example, the heavier-than-air gases that develop in silos may sometimes escape and have harmful effects on humans and animals. Working with animals is in itself not entirely safe: a kick from a horse can cause serious injury.

Solutions to Health Problems

Awareness of the situations that farm women have to confront, which affect their health and that of their families, has given rise to some debate. Solutions for these complex problems are as much the responsibility of governments and of public and community agencies as they are of farmers themselves.

■ Access to Services

To begin with, it would seem important that attempts be made to decentralize medical care in order to ensure access to services in all regions. Some provinces have already adopted measures to discourage doctors from establishing themselves in large centres. In Ontario, doctors who practise in isolated areas are guaranteed a minimum income.[50] British Columbia places a limit on the number of doctors in urban areas.[51] The Quebec government has tried to discourage doctors from setting up practice in Montreal or Quebec City by reducing, in these cities, the basic benefit fees usually granted, and by paying doctors who practise in medically underserviced centres up to 120 per cent of their fees.[52]

When, despite corrective measures, services cannot be offered in rural areas because of a lack of specialists or because of the difficulty of putting certain expensive equipment to productive use, access to these services in urban areas must be facilitated as much as possible. This means transportation and lodging at affordable costs; recommendation 19 in the report on rural women by the Ontario Ministry of Agriculture and Food went so far as to propose that travelling and accommodation expenses be recovered through income tax refunds.[53]

■ Information, Research, Action

Better provision of care in rural areas must be accompanied by improved provision of information to farm women. This information may come from official sources, through programs offered by educational institutions, and also from community groups. It can be disseminated through television, radio, literature, videotapes, or slide shows. Information on birth control should be accessible to adult women, to teenagers in schools, and in centres frequented by these individuals.

Birth itself should be humanized by setting up new alternatives such as home deliveries and birthing rooms. In Quebec, the Cercles des fermières has recommended that the midwives' profession be legally recognized and independently controlled, and that the necessary training be given at the university level.[54] This agency also carried out an activity of benefit to its members during its meeting in August 1985: for one full day, the uterine cancer (Pap) test was offered to all members.

Many fields of research are still to be explored before a more precise measure can be made of the effects of new technology and use of chemical products, particularly with respect to conception, pregnancy, and child development. There is a need for research on the use of nontherapeutic antibiotics in animal feed. The Cercles des fermières also passed the following recommendation at its 1985 meeting:

We recommend that the federal and provincial governmental authorities recognize the potential dangers to human health posed by the use of

nontherapeutic antibiotics in animal feed, and that they allocate the necessary research funds to find an alternative to this practice.[55]
(*translation*)

Through its Health Promotion Program, Health and Welfare Canada is subsidizing projects in several Canadian provinces designed to disseminate information to rural women and to assist them in setting up self-help groups. Of course, the support that women can give each other is also invaluable. Women's health centres have also been established in recent years with the aim of developing approaches more sensitive to the particular interests of women and supportive of their endeavours to maintain control of their bodies. But are these efforts sufficient?

Creation of networks is also seen as necessary. Farm women, like urban women, often lack confidence in themselves; networking enables them to realize that many of their problems are shared by other women. Solidarity leads to group action. Women Today is an Ontario agency formed in precisely this way. Initiated five years ago out of a concern for violence against women, this group is today an articulate voice on the issue of the health of women in rural areas.[56] All local and provincial agencies of this nature help to change ideas and facilitate progress on various fronts.

Because of the lack of specialists in the area of stress, farm women have had to consult urban professionals for treatment of stress. Since these professionals are not familiar with rural life, farm women have found their help unsatisfactory.[57] Workshops on dealing with stress might therefore be valuable alternative solutions to this problem. One association, Women of Unifarm, has been concerned with this problem since 1978. A program for the purpose of outlining the causes of stress, ways of counteracting it, and the existing resources has been offered through workshops in several provinces.

Solutions to Safety Problems

The increase in the number of farm accidents demands concerted attention be given to means of reversing this trend. Here, as in the health area, some measures are the responsibility of the government, others are the concern of farm associations and agencies, and still others require the personal commitment of farmers.

For example, the Ford Motor Company created the Ford Tractor Agricultural Women's Council in 1983. There is no question that the aim of this initiative was to develop new markets for tractor sales. However,

among the questions examined by the committee of Canadian and American farm women was the means to make tractor technology safer. Adjustable seats, addition of steps, better visibility, and a transmission designed to handle more easily were some of the changes recommended. Changes were, in fact, made — but only to the most expensive models. Nonetheless, the long-term impact of this communication between big manufacturers and women consumers should not be underestimated.

The Farm Safety Association (Ontario) has produced a series of excellent fact sheets. Easy to read and presented in an accessible format, these discuss installation of fences around dangerous areas, and deal with noise pollution, stress, first aid, and other topics. Audio-visual presentations have also been assembled by this group. Similar associations exist in Alberta and Saskatchewan, and probably in other provinces. Their educational and informational role is vital. A committee has been estabished in New Brunswick; once it receives funding, it plans to inform the rural population about the use of insecticides and to organize workshops on first aid techniques and other related matters.[58]

There is already abundant documentation on farm safety, but laws are needed to make protective features and wearing of seat belts on tractors compulsory. Distribution of comprehensive information on the risks that farmers run in using certain products and machines is an urgent necessity. People living on family farms or on farms far from hospital and medical centres should be strongly urged to take first aid courses instructing them in artificial respiration, cardiac massage, procedures to stop bleeding, and other techniques. Government departments concerned could develop more audio-visual presentations on these subjects, and make them available to farm and other agencies throughout Canada. These agencies, in turn, should adopt education and information objectives and make full use of the material available.

Information campaigns must be effective if they are to persuade farm workers to adopt safer habits, such as buckling seat belts, wearing protective masks and clothing, and stringent observance of hygienic measures. Safety education of the young has been recognized as a means to nip bad habits in the bud. The regional committee of farm women of Saguenay-Lac St-Jean in Quebec has sought the financial support of an insurance company for a course on accident-prevention for children between 4 and 15 years of age. The women on this committee hope to educate parents through their children. The Farm Safety Association (Ontario) is offering an information package, called Rural Ontario Safety Kit, to elementary schools.

After viewing the film *Play Safe*,[59] which tells the story of ten children who lost limbs in farm accidents, the Women's Institute of Ontario decided to collaborate with Concerned Farm Women to sponsor a pilot child-care project in Bruce County, Ontario. Thanks to a federal goverment grant, they were able to offer services for the modest sum of $1.00 a day.

Regardless of how effective information and prevention may be, work-related accidents will never be totally eliminated. Protection of farmers and farm workers through occupational health and safety laws therefore remains a continuing necessity. To the great disadvantage of the agricultural sector, some provinces do not yet have legislation on farm safety. Thus, there is still a need for action to ensure the passage of necessary laws.

Certainly, it is by learning to "think health and safety" that the most thoroughgoing changes will come. With the requisite tools and support, farm women can be effective agents of change in their milieu.

NEEDS OF WOMEN WHO ARE VICTIMS OF VIOLENCE

Evidence shows that the problem of violence against women is as widespread in rural as it is in urban areas.[60]

> Wife battering, they (rural and farm women) believe, covers all ages, races, income levels, and is as common in rural as in urban areas.[61]

It is probable that violence against women in farm areas is influenced by the same factors as in cities. These may be individual, family, social, or cultural factors. Social and family roles, stress, living conditions, and use of force to settle problems are equally likely to trigger violence in the country as they are in the city.

Despite the fact that the violence women suffer at the hands of their spouses is considered serious and widespread, it would appear that in some areas the question is still rarely discussed in public. "We have barely begun to talk about it," is a frequent refrain. Openness about family violence is closely tied to the level of activity of women's groups in farming areas, as well as to the age of victims. Older women are more susceptible to the belief that battered women deserve to be battered, and that they have brought violence on themselves.[62] These prejudices, still prevalent, suppress discussion, thereby depriving victims of the societal support they need. Furthermore, the small size of rural communities mitigates privacy, making many victims reluctant to seek help, even through anonymous channels.

Though factors leading to violence are similar in rural and urban settings, the fact remains that remedies for the problem are more uneven and less effective in rural areas. Absence of shelters and transition houses, lack of adequate social services, and even unfavourable weather conditions aggravate isolation of victims, undermining their courage to seek solutions. The spouse may engage in surveillance, the telephone is likely to be a party line, and access to a motor vehicle may be restricted. All of these circumstances make discreet communication with the outside world almost impossible.

A problem as complex as violence against women must be attacked on several fronts. Changes in thinking, education, information, dialogue, and services are absolutely necessary. To propel these changes, the right of women to live free from the threat of violence must be entrenched in the values of our society. At present, wife battering is believed to be learned behavior. Society plays an important role in keeping victims passive.[63]

Educational programs should therefore be directed at the general public, at police forces, and at professionals in legal, social, and health services.

There is an urgent need in rural areas for shelters and transition houses adequately funded to offer safety and security for those seeking refuge and for employees. Such centres provide vital support through contact with counsellors and with other women whose experiences are similar.

> Being with other women who have experienced battering helps to break the
> feeling of isolation and self-blame many women experience. This has proved
> to be invaluable in the treatment of battered women.[64]

It has been found that an interval in a shelter may give battered women the necessary support leading to an end to the violence, or may contribute to reducing it.[65]

The network of "safe houses" seems to be gaining strength in Canada. However, this type of temporary refuge in a private home is useful only as an emergency measure, and only insofar as it allows access to a shelter or transition house. In no case should it be regarded or developed as a self-sufficient solution to harbouring women driven from their homes. It should not be forgotten that in rural areas the safe house is not an anonymous place: it is easy for a man to track down his spouse there. In some areas, an agreement is made with the hospital authorities to reserve a bed for any woman in difficulty; this is one safe alternative.

In addition to the shelter network, other services must also be considered. A toll-free telephone line, such as the one now in effect in Manitoba, could, in emergencies, link the farming area to available resources. An attentive ear and judicious advice may enable a battered woman to take the first step in solving her problems.

The violence that women suffer leads to loss of self-confidence. The programs designed for battered women normally deal with this question and for this reason alone are therefore extremely useful.

Government financial assistance, both federal and provincial (depending on the nature of the project), is essential for the survival of shelters and for large-scale education of the population. Such assistance is also necessary for women who do not have enough money to leave their homes when their lives or safety are threatened, and who are not eligible for welfare benefits for the very reason that they are still living with their spouses.

To end the problem of battered women, a whole series of measures therefore must be implemented in both rural and urban areas. Some initiatives that may have an impact on the rural sector are worth examining.

In Manitoba, for instance, a whole series of initiatives, sometimes benefitting both rural and urban areas, has been adopted in aid of victims of conjugal violence. For example:

- an agreement has been concluded with hospital emergency wards and ambulance services regarding services to be offered to battered women;
- a toll-free telephone line is offered province-wide for crisis situations;
- a provincial media campaign to educate the public has been launched;
- non-profit shelters are offered mortgage financing at a preferred rate;
- mediation and anti-violence groups have been subsidized.[66]

In Saskatchewan, the Women's Institute has trained some association members to educate people in rural areas by holding workshops.[67] This type of activity seems to arouse interest in other groups and associations. The Office for the Prevention of Family Violence, Alberta Ministry of Social Services and Community Health, has published a working document entitled *Alberta's Special Report on Family Violence: Ideas for Action*. It deals with financing of shelters, establishment of homes that will take in women for longer periods of time, provision of improved services, etc.[68] In April 1987, the Ontario government announced its intention to more than double its spending on shelters, counselling, and public information campaigns in an effort to stem family violence.[69]

In Quebec, the ministère de la Justice, together with the Bureau du

Solliciteur général and the ministère des Affaires sociales, has recently initiated a policy intended to impress upon police forces and the legal system the fact that beating one's spouse is just as criminal as beating any other person, and does not fall under the category of simple domestic quarrels. Police officers will receive training and will, in turn, become trainers themselves. When a woman is considered in danger, the police officer must lodge a complaint, without having to obtain the victim's consent. The officer will also be required to inform the victim of her rights.

Pressure exerted by women's groups is part and parcel of the concern that has arisen on this subject; this pressure is the best guarantee of the development of a genuine political will to resolve the problem of women who are assaulted by their spouses. This struggle is in itself another prerequisite for equality.

As mentioned earlier, the agricultural sector is also undergoing change. Adaptation to new modes of production, development, administration, and marketing can sometimes proceed smoothly, but most of the time these transitions require specific training for farmers. For example, introduction of new technology generally involves more than reading of an instruction manual. Access to training is as indispensable in agriculture as it is in other advanced industrial sectors. The profitability of the business depends on it. Of course, an understanding of the impact of government decisions on farming is also necessary, and may demand acquisition of special kinds of knowledge.

The value of the work of farm women should not only be a factor in the context of the family business, but should be a priority for agencies promoting or representing farmers' interests, as well as being a key element in defining the role that farm women play within farm businesses. Farm women need to prepare themselves to take full command of their rightful status, because, as expressed so well by Suzanne Dion, women will be of service to the business only by finding their place within it and by being able to carry out their roles effectively.[70]

In Canada, the provinces are responsible for providing for the educational needs of the population. Given the constant change in the workplace, adult education is increasingly vital, both in rural and urban areas. Unfortunately, it has not been possible to discover the proportion of continuing education budgets directed to the rural population, as compared to the urban population. As a result, it is difficult to determine whether the services offered meet existing needs.[71]

According to certain studies intended to establish the training needs of farm women, it appears that a whole range of courses and programs are perceived as necessary. In the Ontario survey on women in rural life, the three subject categories in which women wanted programs were clearly indicative of their desire to be competent on all fronts. The three categories were agricultural courses, home economics courses for better domestic productivity, and personal-improvement courses.[72]

One hundred per cent of the presentations and briefs submitted called for courses in farm management. Farm women are increasingly aware that competent business management is necessary for success. Eighty-eight per cent of the presentations mentioned the importance of legal courses, and 75 per cent the importance of training in production. Other matters, such as estate planning, accounting, farm safety, information, and marketing were brought forward in the majority of the presentations. Among home economics courses, those on arts, crafts, and leisure were most popular, and were rated as important in 75 per cent of presentations. Leadership development topped the personal-improvement courses (46 per cent).[73]

In Quebec, the subjects in which farm women would like training, while not classified in the same way, are in similar areas and indicate the same type of needs.[74] In her paper on the vocational training needs of farm women, Suzanne Dion determined the training needs of farm women by means of an analysis of their situations and the results of a questionnaire distributed to 52,000 Quebec farm women. In this questionnaire, she deliberately combined occupational subjects and personal subjects in order to discover the relative interest of farm women in vocational development.[75] The two vocational areas in which the farm women expressed greatest interest in training were agriculture (49 per cent) and farm economy (48 per cent). Next came personal-improvement subjects, such as crafts (32 per cent), psychology of the couple (32.3 per cent), self-affirmation (21.8 per cent), and self-awareness (21.2 per cent).

The emphasis on the need for courses such as craft techniques suggests more than an interest in hobbies.[76] This is an area in which women are not in competition with their spouses, and which can be justified as enhancing the traditional roles of wife, mother, and housekeeper. Furthermore, in these courses, women are accepted as women, a factor that may account for their popularity. "The possible explanations," writes Suzanne Dion, "emphasize the necessity of working with farm women on such matters as self-image, self-affirmation, and the identity they want to have."[77]

Training most sought after by Quebec farm women is in the subject areas of bookkeeping, administration, and animal care. Research, mechanical work, and greenhouse work are at the bottom of the list.[78]

The resource persons with whom the training needs of farm women were discussed unanimously reported that needs do not substantially differ from one province to another, and that findings in one province can usually serve as a guide to those in another.

Initiatives

Almost everywhere in Canada, programs are offered to farmers by school boards, agricultural technology institutes, universities, and volunteer agencies. However, it is essential to emphasize that farm women need programs specifically designed for them, both because they have some catching up to do in farm education, and because the businesses they are involved in differ from other small- and medium-sized businesses, and require appropriate training and skill.[79]

In Quebec, it has been observed that even though there are adult farm training programs, women participate in them in limited numbers, and that there are various reasons for this. The farm women with the greatest responsibilities and the largest financial commitments seem more motivated. The others plead lack of time, distances to be travelled, the greater importance of their spouse's participation, and, sometimes, the fact that their status does not entitle them to enrol in certain programs.[80]

In a study conducted by the Edmonton section of the Canadian Congress for Learning Opportunities for Women (CCLOW), entitled *In Search of Opportunity*, the researchers delved still further into identification of the factors that generally curtail participation of women in educational programs, and found:

- obstacles of an institutional nature: admission rules, non recognition of experience;
- obstacles of a financial nature: student loans largely dependent on the spouse's income;

and other barriers such as:

- distances to be travelled;
- inadequate counselling services, child-care services that are inaccessible for various reasons (cost, the centres' business hours);
- attitudes toward the social roles of men and women.[81]

Knowing the living conditions of farm women, it is easily seen that constraints hindering women from meeting some of their needs are just as significant where training and education are concerned, and are among the barriers that all women must face. Thus, barriers may prevail over the best of intentions. In both the Ontario survey of the situation of women in rural areas[82] and the study of women in agriculture by the ministère de l'Education du Québec,[83] the conflict between needs expressed and ability to satisfy them has been noted unequivocally. The Ontario report goes so far as to make what seems to the author to be a fundamental point: that this conflict must be resolved if women are to achieve equality in agricultural education, thereby enabling them to make a more meaningful contribution to the farming economy.[84]

From this perspective, there is no doubt of the need for customized training, in terms not only of content but of structure.

The question of how training programs should be oriented so that they facilitate participation of farm women should not overlook the fact that many institutions throughout Canada are already offering information on a great variety of subjects related to agriculture. As mentioned earlier, there are institutions specializing in agricultural education, and regular schools offering their rural clientele programs suited to their concerns.

Offered through the initiative of the Canada Farm Labour Pool in Brandon, with support from Canada Employment and Immigration and the local community college, the Shoal Lake Farm Women Machinery and Safety Course shows how successful such programs can be.[85]

The first six-week "non-traditional part-time course" was recently completed. Offering the course only as an experiment, its organizers were apprehensive about the level of interest that it would draw. They need not have been. Following advertisement of the course, they walked into a preliminary planning meeting to find 38 interested applicants. Class-size limitations meant that less than half (14) of the applicants were able to participate; the remaining women were placed on a waiting list.

The course emphasized safety considerations in operating machinery. According to the instructor, an important feature of the course was to give the women an understanding of how things work, rather than just to demonstrate what they do.[86] Operation and servicing of tractors, small engines, grain dryers, water pumps, and aeration systems were taught. Women who took the course also learned to operate combines, hook up hydraulic systems, service cars, and handle anhydrous ammonia.

Applicants to the program were relatively young, typically were former clerical workers, nurses or teachers, and had been involved in farming for five to seven years. Their need for the course was described by one student, who, upon being told that there was not much to the course, other than what her husband could show her, replied, "Are you kidding? I usually get stuck on the machine in the middle of some crisis — when it's time to 'go'. There's never any time to learn and he thinks it's so straightforward it hardly needs an explanation."[87] In general, the women had two principal reasons for taking the course. Some wanted to become more involved in farming; others, who had worked on the farm, wanted to improve their skills. Emphasis on confidence-building and on safety are aspects of the courses particularly appreciated by graduates. In turn, the teachers enjoy the women's desire to learn. As one instructor said, "I'd rather teach 10 women than 5 men anyday. They're here to learn and there's no messing around."[88] Success of the first course prompted sponsorship of another in Minnedosa, Manitoba. Again, applications exceeded available spaces.

Provincial ministries of agriculture are also very active in this area. In Quebec, the ministère de l'Agriculture, des Pêcheries et de l'Alimentation, through the agency of the Bureau de la répondante à la condition féminine, has just launched a plan of action called *Du partage des tâches au partage des pouvoirs*.[89] The general aim of this plan is to develop the programs necessary to ensure farm women a visible and full role in the agriculture of Quebec.[90] One of the goals of the plan is to promote the vocational development of farm women through programs based on their specific needs and offered by various educational institutions. Other programs are also planned on subjects ranging from leadership training to credit information, laws, etc.

In addition to these programs, all those arising from initiatives of farm women themselves should be mentioned. Almost everywhere in Canada, farm women's associations distribute information on their rights and legal status. They also do a great deal of educational work on many questions of the sort dealt with in this study. Farm women play an increasingly important role in farmers' groups, and some of the training they want is intended specifically to permit them to assume their full and rightful place in those groups: leadership, parliamentary procedures, and public speaking are just some of the subjects in which interest has been expressed.

Within the Union des producteurs agricoles du Québec (UPA), for example, women have united in order to present their demands more forcefully. One provincial committee, as well as a number of regional committees, have been set up. Meanwhile, Women for the Survival of Agriculture has designed courses specifically for women in agriculture.[91]

In Alberta, the Rural Education and Development Association (REDA) produces and distributes literature on subjects ranging from free trade with the United States, to the role of women as community leaders, to how to take over after the death of a spouse and co-worker.

Like the other issues discussed in this article, that of training requires a good deal of imagination and open-mindedness in order to satisfy existing needs. Training can, and sometimes must, be given in traditional classes and workshops organized by various associations to better reach people in their own milieu. For example, farm management unions developing in Quebec operate on a system whereby a certain number of farmers (about 50) form a group and hire a farming consultant. The consultant helps them to plan their production and provides information on all aspects of farm management, as well as on subjects such as the government deficit, free trade, and interest rates — in short, on everything that affects their economic situation. However, a farming concern is entitled to only one vote in the union; this limits participation of women, who nonetheless have the opportunity to work closely with the consultant. The unions are affiliated with the Union des producteurs agricoles.[92]

New communications technology can also offer interesting means to disseminate information and training desired by farm women. For example, more and more families own a tape-recorder or VCR; this means that cassettes can be recorded and distributed more easily, at affordable prices. A cassette can be listened to as often as necessary and at convenient times of the day or week; to complement this information, all that would be needed is a resource person available to answer questions about unresolved problems. Community radio and television could also play an important role.

CONCLUSION

It is clear that farm women are able to formulate creative solutions and to take the initiative to help themselves. Thus, they must be the first to be consulted in order to ensure the formation of productive structures and programs.

Meeting the needs of farm women will always depend to a large extent on the political will of various levels of government. For example, if the objective of government is to develop large-scale farming industry to the detriment of small-and medium-sized concerns, the battle for the survival of the family business has only just begun. Because the quality of farm life is closely linked to the family farm, this is an issue of primary importance to farm women. In this and other issues, the orientation of agriculture in Canada must reflect all of the values at stake, including those of farm women who make such an important contribution.

1. Marie-Claire Dumas, "S.O.S. des femmes de terre," *Châtelaine*, vol. 26, no. 4 (April 1985), p. 140.

2. Rosaline Ledoux, "Le travail des mères doit bénéficier aux filles," *La Terre de chez nous*, vol. 56, no. 41 (1985). Mrs. Ledoux reports Suzanne Dion's comments. (*La Terre de chez nous* is a weekly produced by the Union des producteurs agricoles du Québec (UPA) and distributed to some 50,000 subscribers.)

3. Lois Sweet, "Voices of Rural Women Heard at Last," *Toronto Star* (July 7, 1984), p. L3.

4. Women for the Survival of Agriculture, *What Are You Worth? A Study of the Economic Contribution of Eastern Ontario Farm Women to the Family Farm Enterprise*, submitted to the Second National Farm Women's Conference, Charlottetown, Prince Edward Island, November 21-24, 1985, p. 6.

5. Gisèle Ireland, *The Farmer Takes a Wife* (Chesley: Concerned Farm Women, 1983), p. 47.

6. See the discussion in Pamela Smith's article.

7. Ireland, *The Farmer Takes a Wife*, p. 41.

8. Preliminary results of survey distributed to the majority of Quebec farm homes through the newspaper *La Terre de chez nous*, vol. 55, no. 50 (1985). Information obtained from the Bureau de la répondante à la condition féminine of the ministère de l'Agriculture, des Pêcheries et de l'Alimentation du Québec. See also the study conducted in Saskatchewan by the Sample Survey and Data Bank Unit, *Day Care Needs and Demands in Saskatchewan* (Regina: University of Regina, 1978).

9. The Special Committee on Child Care was established in November 1985. It has power of recommendation to the House of Commons.

10. Women for the Survival of Agriculture, *What Are You Worth?*, p. 29.

11. Molly McGhee, *Women in Rural Life: The Changing Scene* (Toronto: Ministry of Agriculture and Food, 1984), p. 17.

12. Manitoba Advisory Council on the Status of Women, *Some Concerns of Rural and Farm Women* (Winnipeg: 1984), p. 3.

13. Canada, Task Force on Child Care, *Report of the Task Force on Child Care* (Ottawa: Supply and Services Canada, 1986), p. 97. (This task force was formed in May 1984 and issued its report in March 1986.)

14. Dianne Harkin, "Who's Minding the Kids?", *Canada Poultryman*, vol. 71, no. 10 (October 1984), pp. 42-43.

15. Preliminary results of survey distributed through *La Terre de chez nous*.

16. Wellington Rural Child Care Network, *Proceedings from Working Together for Change* (Guelph, Ontario: 1985), p. 21.

17. *Ibid.*, p. 9.

18. Luisa D'Amato, "Plans to Boost Child Care Unveiled,"

Kitchener-Waterloo Record (September 19, 1985), p. 83.

19. Women for the Survival of Agriculture, *What Are You Worth?*, p. 31.

20. Wellington Rural Child Care Network, *Proceedings from Working Together for Change*, pp. 4-5.

21. *Ibid.*, pp. 6-7.

22. Canada, Task Force on Child Care, *Report*, p. 64.

23. Women for the Survival of Agriculture, *What Are You Worth?*, p. 30.

24. Canada, Task Force on Child Care, *Report*, p. 373.

25. Dumas, "S.O.S. des femmes de Terre," p. 140.

26. Lois L. Ross, "Farm Women: The Unrecognized Resource," in *Prairie Lives: the Changing Face of Farming* (Toronto: Between the Lines, 1985), p. 42.

27. McGhee, *Women in Rural Life.*

Manitoba Advisory Council on the Status of Women, *Some Concerns of Rural and Farm Women.*

28. Anita Fochs Heller, *Health and Home: Women as Health Guardians* (Ottawa: Canadian Advisory Council on the Status of Women, 1986).

29. Gail Lem, "Distribution of Medical Practitioners Causing Problems," *Globe and Mail* (June 13, 1983), p. B-18.

30. Data obtained from the Canadian Medical Association, March 1986. (Number of physicians by province, by specialty, and for certain rural regions for the year of 1982) and Canada, Statistics Canada, *Population: Age, Sex and Marital Status* (Ottawa: Supply and Services Canada, 1982), 1981 Census of Canada, catalogue no. 92-901, for the population distribution by province.

31. Information obtained in telephone interviews.

32. J.D. Hatcher and F.M.M. White, *Task Force on Chemicals in the Environment and Human Reproductive Problems in New Brunswick* (Halifax: Faculty of Medicine, Dalhousie University, 1985), pp. 107-108.

33. *Ibid.*, p. 108.

34. Ontario Task Force on Health and Safety in Agriculture, *Report* (Ontario: Ministry of Agriculture and Food; Ministry of Labour, 1985), Appendix 3, p. 10.

35. Ontario Task Force on Health and Safety in Agriculture, *Report*, Appendix 3, p. 10.

36. Nancy Miller Chenier, *Reproductive Hazards At Work: Men, Women and the Fertility Gamble* (Ottawa: Canadian Advisory Council on the Status of Women, 1982), p. 30.

37. Ontario Task Force on Health and Safety in Agriculture, *Report*, Appendix 3, p. 12.

38. Maureen Trotter, "Living on the Land," *Kinesis* (September 1984), p. 12.

39. Ontario Task Force on Health and Safety in Agriculture, *Report*, Appendix 3, p. 20.

40. Peter R. Boisseau, "Farmer's Lung: It's finally being diagnosed by New Brunswick doctors," *The Times-Transcript*, vol. 2, no. 239 (October 1983).

41. Farm Safety Association, *Noise: Sound Without Value*, fact sheet no. FF007 (Guelph: 1985).

42. Ireland, *The Farmer Takes a Wife*,
p. 51.

    Women of Unifarm, *Stresses in the
    Farm Family Unit* (Edmonton,
    Alberta: 1978), p. 9.

43. Mary Jane Lipkin, co-ordinator,
    Status of Rural Women Project,
    "The Socio-economic Status of Farm
    Women: an Overview," *First
    National Farm Women's Conference
    Background Papers*, Ottawa,
    December 2-4, 1980.

44. Linda Craig, "Factors Associated
    with Stress in Farm Women," paper
    presented to the Canadian Sociology
    and Anthropology Association at
    the Learned Societies Conference,
    University of Guelph, June 6-9,
    1984, pp. 9-10.

45. Ontario Task Force on Health and
    Safety in Agriculture, *Report*,
    p. 141.

46. *Ibid.*, p. 38.

47. Harkin, "Who's Minding the Kids?",
    pp. 42-43.

48. Ontario Department of Agriculture,
    Farm Accident Survey (Toronto:
    1960), cited in Ontario Task Force on
    Health and Safety in Agriculture,
    Report, p. 55.

49. Ruth Benedict, "Sorry, No Kids
    Allowed!," *Farm Woman News*,
    vol. 15, no. 9 (September 1985), p. 17.

50. Lem, "Distribution of Medical
    Practitioners Causing Problems,"
    p. B-18.

51. Information obtained from the
    Canadian Health Coalition.

52. Lem, "Distribution of Medical
    Practitioners Causing Problems,"
    p. B-18.

53. McGhee, *Women in Rural Life*, p. 36.

54. Cercles de fermières du Québec,

    Comité exécutif provincial, *Congrès
    Provincial 1985: Recommandation.*

55. *Ibid.*

56. Susan Hundertmark, "Rural
    Feminism," *Healthsharing*, vol. 7,
    no. 1 (winter 1985), p. 15.

57. Ireland, *The Farmer Takes a Wife*,
    p. 57.

58. Information obtained in telephone
    interviews.

59. *Play Safe*, film produced by the War
    Amputations of Canada and
    available to persons and groups
    interested in safety.

60. Women for the Survival of
    Agriculture, *What Are You Worth?*,
    p. 34.

61. Manitoba Advisory Council on the
    Status of Women, *Some Concerns of
    Rural and Farm Women*, p. 6.

62. McGhee, *Women in Rural Life*, p. 34.

    Women for the Survival of
    Agriculture, *What Are You Worth?*,
    p. 36.

63. Women for the Survival of
    Agriculture, *What Are You Worth?*,
    p. 36.

64. Saskatchewan Battered Women's
    Advocacy Network, *Services and
    Shelter for Battered Women in
    Saskatchewan* (Regina, Sask. s.d.)

65. Lee Chalmers, "Wife Battering:
    Social and Physical Isolation and
    Appropriate Counteracting
    Strategies," paper presented at the
    annual conference of the Canadian
    Research Institute for the
    Advancement of Women, Saskatoon,
    November 1985.

66. Results of telephone interviews.

67. *Ibid.*

68. Alberta Social Services and

Community Health, *Alberta's Special Report on Family Violence: Ideas for Action* (Edmonton, Alberta: 1985).

69. "Ontario to double spending in drive to reduce wife-beating," *Toronto Star*, April 16, 1987.

70. Suzanne Dion, "Les besoins de formation professionnelle des agricultrices," Master's Thesis, University of Montreal, 1985, p. 96.

71. Results of conversations with the Canadian Association for University Continuing Education.

72. McGhee, *Women in Rural Life*, pp. 42-43.

73. *Ibid.*

74. Quebec, ministère de l'Education, Direction générale de l'Education des adultes, *Femmes en agriculture* (Quebec: 1984), pp. 18-20.

75. Dion, "Les besoins de formation professionnelle des agricultrices," p. 86.

76. *Ibid.*, p. 87.

77. *Ibid.*

78. *Ibid.*, p. 64.

79. Quebec, ministère de l'Education, *Femmes en agriculture*, p. 15.

80. *Ibid.*, p. 14-15.

81. Women's Educational Research Project, *In Search of Opportunity: a Preliminary Evaluation of Learning Opportunities for Women in Alberta* (Edmonton, Alberta: Canadian Congress for Learning Opportunities for Women, Edmonton Chapter, 1984), pp. 47-48.

82. McGhee, *Women in Rural Life*, p. 40.

83. Quebec, ministère de l'Education, *Femmes en agriculture*, pp. 18-20.

84. McGhee, *Women in Rural Life*, p. 40.

85. Darell Nesbitt, "Farm Women Learn Farming Techniques," *Shoal Lake Star* (March 19, 1986), p. 9.

86. Peter Misanchuk, personal interview, 1985.

87. *Ibid.*

88. *Ibid.*

89. Quebec, ministère de l'Agriculture, des Pêcheries et de l'Alimentation, Bureau de la répondante à la condition féminine, *From Sharing the Work to Sharing the Power: Three Year Plan* (Quebec: 1986).

90. Quebec, ministère de l'Agriculture, des Pêcheries et de l'Alimentation, news release on the occasion of the publication of *From Sharing the Work to Sharing the Power: Three Year Plan*.

91. Women for the Survival of Agriculture, *What Are You Worth?*, p.38.

92. Information obtained in telephone interviews.

Farm Women: Obtaining Legal and Economic Recognition of Their Work

by Michelle Boivin

2 TABLE OF CONTENTS

ACKNOWLEDGEMENTS

The author wishes to thank Sophie Benazet for her invaluable assistance in researching and writing this article. Readers are asked to note that all research was completed in March 1986.

Michelle Boivin

INTRODUCTION

When discussing farm women and the need to recognize their work, it is first necessary to define the terms of reference. Who is a farm woman? Is it enough simply to marry a farmer, or to live with him, to become a farm woman?[1] What about the full-time teacher, or part-time cashier, who is the legal or common-law wife of a farmer?[2] Must a farm woman also perform farming duties, like feeding animals or driving a tractor?[3] Should activities relating to the enterprise as a whole, such as contributing funds, keeping books, and doing the ordering be taken into account?[4] Is a farm woman exclusively someone who is the head of a farm enterprise (independent worker), a co-operator, or an employee of the farmer?[5] Obviously the term *farm woman* brings to mind all of these images simultaneously.

If the problem is considered from the point of view of the duties performed, and thus of the work to be recognized, then clearly the theme of this study touches on all of the problems facing women. A farm woman, whether married or living common-law with a farmer, generally has responsibility for household work and child care. Recognition of domestic work is of concern to nearly every woman. The traditional legal position is that this is a private problem, which involves only the couple and may be settled on the basis of the legal obligations arising out of the marriage and the applicable matrimonial property regime.

Moreover, recognition of the work done by farm women as co-operators is a part of the broader struggle of women working with their husbands in family enterprises, or *co-worker wives*. In law, this situation is seen as a function of the legal status of the enterprise and the position of the co-worker wife within it (e.g., employee, partner, shareholder).

A farm woman who is the head of an enterprise must also deal with extremely persistent prejudices in our society: "A woman can't operate a farm alone; the work is too hard!" This is a popular impression — that farming demands hard physical labour far beyond the strength and stamina of most women.

If the work of farm women is to be recognized, they must change their self-image, and their definition of work. As Suzanne Dion put it:

> Some women operate machinery, some tend to the cows, some act as receptionists, secretaries, accountants, researchers, labour relations officers, personnel managers, sanitary technicians, mechanics, truck-drivers, salespeople, public relations officers, planners, buyers, and so on. *They call this "helping out, running errands, answering the phone."*[6]

Farm women themselves tend to underestimate their contributions, however essential, and fail to see themselves as actual producers.[7]

For many people, awareness of the *woman problem* in general and the *farm woman problem* in particular arose very recently; one significant event was the creation of the Royal Commission on the Status of Women in Canada (the Bird Commision) which filed its report in 1970.[8] Initial awareness of the problem came as a result of a number of socio-economic factors, all of which revealed the victimization and the poverty of women as a group, whether they be workers, single-parent heads of families, or the elderly and unattached.[9] But it was the 1975 Murdoch case[10] that brought to the attention of Canadians as a whole the dilemma facing women in general, and farm women in particular. It will be recalled that, in this case, Irene Murdoch claimed in her divorce petition to be entitled to one-half of the land and other property used in the joint operation of a farm. The evidence revealed that Mrs. Murdoch had indeed actively participated in operating the farm for 20 years, taking on alone all the duties of the farm during her husband's extended absences. The Supreme Court of Canada nevertheless refused to give Mrs. Murdoch her one-half share, on the grounds that she had done only "the work done by any ranch wife." This scandalous phrase mobilized the whole female population.

In the past, of course, there have been a number of associations originally designed to bring farm women together, such as the Cercles de fermières du Québec and the Federated Women's Institutes of Canada in the other provinces. Now, however, there is a proliferation of other groups with more political goals and more radical positions.[11] These groups and associations have been working to raise the consciousness of the public at large, and of women in particular, through publication of some incisive studies.

Background documents for the First National Farm Women's Conference, held in Ottawa in 1980, and the natural forum provided by that event gave farm women a chance to identify some of their common problems: lack of general recognition of their work, both in food production and in caring for children and family; lack of time and training; lack of power and influence over the future of agriculture as a whole; and especially lack of legal recognition of their work.[12]

At the Second National Conference of Farm Women held in Prince Edward Island in 1985, the status of women was discussed within the context of the economic crisis. Five years of a cycle that had hit industry and agriculture particularly hard had changed the direction of the discussions:

> We must admit that this economic crisis has not created new problems for farm women. It has simply highlighted them.

> If anything has changed in terms of power, it is that in situations which have become difficult, women have become aware of the small amount of power they do possess.[13]

Some of the demands put forward[14] have remained relevant to farm women, particularly the demand that farm women, like all co-worker wives, must have financial independence and rights to the farm operation. Significant reforms have come out of these demands. Among the most important accomplishments of recent years is family law reform, particularly in the area of matrimonial property regimes, first in Quebec in 1970 and later in the common law provinces.[15]

Another significant legislative victory has undeniably been amendment of tax laws to permit deduction of the salary paid as an employee of a spouse (in a sole-proprietorship enterprise) or of a company owned by the spouse.[16] In addition, the discretionary power of the Minister of National Revenue to attribute the income of a spouse who is a partner in an enterprise to the other spouse, and to tax the latter on the income, has been removed.[17] This is an important reform, because it indicates the intention of Parliament to no longer necessarily identify the economic unit with the family unit. Clearly, there is yet a long way to go, but this is one step toward financial independence, and one more argument that can be used in negotiating with husbands.

Also worthy of mention are other legislative changes, of somewhat less importance to farm women, which were made to the Canada Pension Plan,[18] and the *1985 Divorce Act*, finally permitting "no-fault" divorce;[19] and the new measures to facilitate collection of support payments.[20] Parliament made these changes in response to demands by women. At the socio-political level, the appointment of someone responsible for the status of women within the Quebec ministère de l'Agriculture in 1984, and the creation of the Bureau de la répondante à la condition féminine in 1986, also mark an important step toward recognition of women in Quebec's agricultural sector.

But let us return to the original question. Does Canada today have institutions capable of providing economic and legal recognition of all forms of work done by farm women? Economic recognition of work generally takes the form of income, or a right to ownership of property. Legal recognition of work (or the legal status of a worker) is determined by the existence of property rights or the methods of performing or being paid for work, and sometimes even by the legal status of the enterprise in question. For this reason, the present possibilities for legal and economic recognition of the work done by farm women will be considered first, by examining in sequence avenues for obtaining access to income or property rights, depending on the legal form of the farm enterprise. Next, matrimonial property regimes and succession legislation, which may be seen as avenues for obtaining deferred access to income or property rights, will be discussed. Then the various obstacles to recognition, particularly the difficulties of obtaining credit and the traditional ways of passing on land, will be examined. Finally, potential solutions to these problems will be considered.

CURRENT POSSIBILITIES FOR ACCESS TO INCOME AND PROPERTY RIGHTS

Immediate Access

The possibilities of recognizing a farm woman's contribution to the operation of the farm through income or property rights are, to a large extent, determined by the legal form of the enterprise and the legal status of the woman within this structure. For this reason, a brief summary of the legal rules applying to the status of employee, partner, and shareholder-director follows.

■ Employee

The legal concept of *employee* generally is "a person who works for an employer and for remuneration."[21] The essential element of this definition is the subordinate relationship: the work is done *for* someone, in accordance with instructions given.[22] An employee is a person who carries out orders received, and who may be dismissed for insubordination. In the power relationship, the employee's position is inferior to that of the employer, and it is for this reason that legislators have enacted laws to protect employees by compelling employers to respect certain minimum standards.[23]

The status of employee generally brings with it certain benefits, including the right to receive income (wages or salary),[24] the right to vacation pay,[25] the right to contest an unlawful dismissal,[26] and so on. In addition, an employee may participate in benefit plans such as unemployment insurance, maternity leave, and the Canada Pension Plan or Régime des rentes du Québec, as the case may be. An employee may also claim tax deductions for child care,[27] and may contribute to a registered retirement savings plan (RRSP) up to 18 per cent of her "earned income."[28]

Would it therefore be advantageous for a co-worker farm wife to become an employee, regardless of the form of the enterprise? Clearly, she would then receive an income, so that she would have some financial independence and the opportunity to own property through her own earnings. Unfortunately, however, she would not be entitled to most benefits. In fact, under certain provisions,[29] farm operations (and their employees) can now be exempted from universal pension plans, and are almost inevitably exempted from unemployment insurance provisions,[30] and from other benefits, such as maternity leave.

Moreover, the difficulty that a farm woman might have in negotiating a salary with her husband, in spite of the fact that amendments to the *Income Tax Act* have made some changes more attractive, should not be underestimated. In some cases, to demand "all of a sudden" that she be paid for the services she had, until then, provided free of charge might jeopardize the relationship itself. There is also no specific legal recourse permitting someone who provides services to her spouse without pay to obtain payment.[31] The difficulty is evidentiary: how does one prove that there is a labour contract between spouses? There is often not even a proper oral contract, but rather a habit, a practice of a division of labour that has simply arisen. Furthermore, the dividing line between productive duties necessary for maintenance of the farm and other duties in the household is not always clear. And then there is another problem: the fact that the woman received a salary, however low it may have been, could be interpreted as showing that she received full payment for the services rendered, so that she would have no right to share in the profits of the enterprise, even if her contribution greatly exceeded the salary she received.

In Quebec, as in the rest of Canada, only 20 per cent of co-worker farm wives receive a salary.[32] A study conducted in Quebec in 1984 by the Association des femmes collaboratrices du Québec revealed that in 1.7 per cent of the cases, the salaries of farm women amounted to less than $100 per week; 14.8 per cent received $101 to $200; and 1.7 per cent received $210 and over.[33] It should be added that fewer than 15 per cent of husbands drew a regular salary in farm enterprises.[34] Another interesting fact was that 82 per cent of co-worker wives in incorporated enterprises received a salary, as compared to percentages varying from 20 to 33.3 per cent in other forms of enterprise.[35] Ruth Rose-Lizée suggests the following explanation:

> There is a more formal structure in an incorporated enterprise, and so it is not surprising that in such a case the couple will also choose to formalize the wife's relationship with the enterprise.[36]

However, it may also be that some women intuitively feel that taking on the status of employee would confirm that their position is inferior, and that this does not indeed reflect their daily lives. As one farm woman put it:

> Whether she has a marriage contract or buys the farm, I hope to see a woman become an owner or shareholder on the same footing as her husband. She will no longer feel like a servant, or the hired hand. *But to give the wife a salary — I'm not in favour of that. If she takes a salary, the wife loses her place as her husband's equal.*[37] *(emphasis added.)*

■ Partner

Status as a partner is clearly dependent on the enterprise being a legal partnership. A farm woman who is a partner has all the rights and benefits provided in the partnership agreement governing the enterprise: she participates in profits and losses as provided in the agreement, subject to the following comments with respect to liability to third parties.

There is no legal requirement as to the specific form of the partnership agreement. Thus, the agreement may be oral; then the difficulty arises in providing evidence of the agreement when things go wrong. Let us not harbour any illusions: as long as the relationship is going well, an oral partnership agreement providing for a 50% share does not present problems; but when the marriage or the relationship (in common-law situations) breaks down, it is difficult to prove after the fact that the parties had the mutual intention of dividing the profits equally. It is not enough to state and to prove that one did the work: a judge may decide that the woman was working as a volunteer, or that her work was simply a voluntary contribution to household responsibilities.

Are these evidentiary difficulties insurmountable? The decision in *Beaudoin-Daigneault* v. *Richard* would indicate that they are not.[38] The facts were as follows: the parties, who had been cohabiting for two years, decided in 1973 to purchase a farm and to take up residence on it. Both spouses signed the offer to purchase, but only Mr. Richard signed the deed of sale and the mortgage, thereby becoming the sole legal owner of the land. However, they shared the expenses of maintaining and improving the house, as well as the farm duties "according to their respective strength and abilities."[39] In the spring of 1978, Mr. Richard forced Ms. Daigneault out of the house, and she brought an action alleging dissolution of the partnership and claiming division of the partnership property, which had a value of about $60,000.

The Honourable Judge Tôth, who heard the action at trial, found that there was a partnership agreement and allowed the action. This decision was then reversed by the Quebec Court of Appeal. The following passage from the decision issued by Judge Monet should be noted:

> Then, not surprisingly, the respondent did just what most women who live on farms do: she kept a vegetable garden and did some other work, for example, clearing stones from some parts of the land. In 1973, very little work was done. In 1974, the hay was not cut, but was sold "standing." The fact that at some point the respondent hung wallpaper in one room in the house, paid for a subscription to a special television service and changed a ceiling light fixture at her own expense *is of little significance*. The question that concerns us here is whether or not the spouses had entered into a partnership agreement?[40] *(emphasis added.)*

The decision of the Court of Appeal was ultimately reversed by the Supreme Court on the grounds that the Court of Appeal had exceeded its jurisdiction by substituting its own opinion on questions of fact for that of the trial judge.[41] As a result, Ms. Daigneault won her case.

However, there is an undeniable advantage for a farm woman in having a written partnership contract. It provides secure legal and economic recognition for her work in the realm of commercial rather than family law. In commercial law, there is no assumption that one person would make a gift of her services and property to another person. A partnership agreement offers much more flexibility, and puts the partners on an equal footing, even if their contributions and shares of the profits are unequal. It is also noted that a farm woman may be an employee of a partnership in which her husband and other people are partners.

■ Shareholder-Director of a Company

What advantage does a company offer to a farm woman? In a company, a woman may have dual status. Any capital that she contributes to the company may be in the form of a loan to the company, or it may be in return for issuance of shares of a corresponding value. Shares entitle the holder to participate in the management and profits of the enterprise. As well, the farm woman and her husband may both be elected as directors of the company, and on the board of directors each person is entitled to one vote, regardless of the number of shares he or she holds. Both spouses may also be employees of the company that operates the farm, and the company is considered a separate entity in law. Even if the spouses receive unequal salaries, the fact that they are both employees of the same entity in which both have an interest as an *owner* will, to some extent, remedy the problem of inequality produced if the wife is an employee.[42]

It should be added, however, that a wife who receives a salary from a company is not entitled to receive benefits under government plans if her husband, or the couple together, owns 40% or more of the issued shares.

An additional advantage of incorporating the enterprise is that some property, notably the family home, may be sheltered in the event of bankruptcy. The property of shareholders is legally separate from the property of the company. Anyone who personally guarantees a debt of the company will of course lose the benefit of this protection. It should be noted, however, that in this situation it is almost impossible to dissociate the family home from the farm when there is a sale or transfer.

Although a corporate structure appears at first to be complex, it nevertheless offers the advantage of flexibility and familiarity among professionals and judges. It is therefore easier for a co-worker wife to predict the legal consequences of any given action. The formality of the company's structure will also force the various participants to become more aware of their situation. But more importantly, the company, as a distinct legal entity, will intervene between the co-worker spouses, and the specificity of the rules governing the company will relegate the marital relationship to the background. Thus, for example, commercial law offers a whole range of remedies for the minority shareholder, regardless of whether he or she is (or was) the legal or common-law spouse of the majority shareholder.[43]

It should also be noted that spouses may enter into a shareholder agreement to provide for transfers of shares, including share prices, in the event of a breakdown of the relationship as a result of divorce or death. As well, unanimous shareholder agreements may restrict the powers of the board of directors and provide better protection for minority share- holders.

It is evident that the law today offers a multiplicity of options to farm women who want concrete, immediate recognition of their work. They may gain this by obtaining an income in the form of a salary, a partnership interest, or dividends and property rights in the form of personal title or shares in an incorporated farm enterprise.

Indirect or Deferred Access

Among the avenues available to farm women seeking financial independence and the economic and political power these bring, two other potential sources of income and property rights must also be considered: division of the matrimonial property regime; and gifts or testamentary legacies, or the devolution of property from the estate when the deceased has not written a will (intestate succession).

Matrimonial Property Regimes

The primary objective of matrimonial property regimes is to determine the rights and obligations of the spouses as between themselves, and to govern their financial relations. It is imperative that all women who are thinking of marrying, including, of course, farm women, carefully select their matrimonial property regime, each woman taking into consideration her own particular circumstances. This is the *only way at present* that she can obtain legal and economic recognition, even if it is deferred, of the duties that take up a large part of her life: child care and household work. Society as a whole, and the law in particular, do not recognize this as work in itself,[44] and the wise and informed woman should create her own opportunities to obtain payment from her husband by judiciously choosing her matrimonial property regime. It is for this reason that the choice of regime is so important to the wife-to-be, while it is of less concern to her partner.

As already noted, the upheaval brought about by the *Murdoch*[45] case provoked a general rise in public awareness, the natural outcome being that the matrimonial property regimes in every province in Canada were reformed.[46] These reforms managed to reconcile two fundamentally contradictory concepts: the independence and the equality of each spouse within a marriage considered to be a common enterprise.[47] It should be noted here that every province in Canada opted for a regime providing for community of property for certain property, with joint management and division deferred to dissolution of the regime as a result of cessation of cohabitation, divorce, death, or a voluntary change in the regime, as the case may be. An exhaustive study of all these regimes is clearly beyond the scope of this study, but the regimes provided for in Saskatchewan, Ontario, and Quebec law will be briefly described, followed by discussion of the choices offered in certain typical situations. Why these provinces in particular? Sakatchewan was chosen because its matrimonial property regime closely resembles that of the other provinces, while retaining its own interesting peculiarities; Ontario, because changes have recently been made to its matrimonial property law, and at this point the provisions for division of property go further than those in any other province; and Quebec, because there has always been equal division of property under the community property regime, which was replaced by the community of acquests in 1970, the first of the modern reforms.

■ Saskatchewan

The *Matrimonial Property Act*,[48] enacted on January 1, 1980, was designed to recognize the equality of the partners in a marriage: both spouses are jointly responsible for household duties, and each must contribute, financially or otherwise, to the needs of the family.[49] Accordingly, in the event of dissolution, each spouse is entitled to an equal share of the family property.[50] All property is considered family property except for real property owned before the marriage and gifts or inheritances received during the marriage.[51] A judge has discretion to order unequal division only if equal division of family property would lead to an unfair or inequitable result.[52] There are a number of criteria designed to guide the judge in exercising this discretion, including the length of time the spouses cohabited, the time that has elapsed since the separation, the date the property was acquired, and interests of third parties in the family property.[53] In a recent decision, *Donkin v. Bugoy*, the Supreme Court of Canada held that, once an application for division has been properly made, the subsequent death of the spouse seeking division, and the provisions of his or her will (Mrs. Donkin had disinherited her husband and son) are not extraordinary circumstances that would permit the judge to disregard the rule of equal division.[54]

There are also specific provisions that apply to the matrimonial home. It is already protected by the *Homestead Act*,[55] which provides that a wife's consent must be obtained for any transfer; now the matrimonial home must be divided equally, unless the court finds that there are extraordinary circumstances in light of the above-mentioned criteria.[56]

The Act formally prohibits the court from considering the conduct of the spouses, unless financial loss resulted directly from such conduct.[57] The court may also refuse to consider a contract between the spouses providing for division of property if it finds the contract to be unfair.[58] The Act also provides measures to protect one spouse against another who wishes to dispose of his or her property in order to evade the provisions of the *Matrimonial Property Act*, including a court order prohibiting disposition of the property in question.[59]

■ Ontario

The *Family Law Reform Act* of 1978[60] recognized that spouses contribute equally to the property used by the family, which was referred to as *family assets*, that is, any property used by the family, such as furniture, car, family home, cottage, and so on. Only these assets were normally to be divided into equal shares in the event that cohabitation ceased. However, largely because of the limited definition of *family assets*, the situation still remained inequitable for women in the home.

For this reason, Ontario again changed the matrimonial property regime with *An Act to Revise the Family Law Reform Act*.[61] This new Act ensures that spouses and their contributions will be treated equally.[62] It also affirms the principle that each spouse is entitled to one half of the property acquired between the date of the marriage and the date of separation. The concept of *family property* is expanded to include income from property belonging to one of the spouses before the marriage and any increase in the value of such property during the marriage, the value of pension credits accumulated by the spouses (including the employer's contributions), income from gifts or inheritances, any increase in value during the marriage, and so on.[63] Preferential treatment is given to the matrimonial home, which has always been subject to equal division, regardless of the time and circumstances of acquisition or the person in whose name title is held.[64]

The procedure for division provides for an evaluation, normally on the date on which the separation became final, of all property owned by each spouse, and deduction of all debts relating to such property (for example, mortgages) in order to determine the "net family property" of the spouse who owns them. Any disparity in the value of the property in relation to the property of the other spouse will result in an equalizing payment by one spouse to the other, which may be spread over a maximum period of ten years and may be secured by a charge on the property of the debtor spouse.[65]

The court has very limited discretionary power to deviate from a 50-

50 division. A judge may use this power only when he or she is of the opinion that equal division of net family property would be unacceptable after considering certain factors set out in the Act, such as reckless depletion of property by one of the spouses, or that the share would be disproportionately large in relation to a period of cohabitation less than five years.[66]

The principle set out in the Act also applies to family and farm enterprises. Thus, a farm that was acquired and operated during the marriage will be subject to equal division. However, if the farm belonged to one of the spouses before marriage or if one of them inherited it during the marriage, only the increase in value and income will be divided. At the time of division, the farm will remain the property of the spouse who has title, but the court may order special measures for equalization payments over time. In the event that a cash payment would inevitably entail the sale of a business or farm, or seriously impair its operation, the judge may order that one spouse pay to the other a share of the profits from the business or farm, or issue or transfer to the other spouse shares in an incorporated enterprise.[67]

It should be added that the spouses may opt out of the provisions of the Act, except with respect to the provisions concerning the matrimonial home, by signing a marriage contract or separation agreement.[68] There is also provision for making a "cohabitation agreement" governing the financial relationship and support obligations of common-law spouses, and their right to direct the education and moral training of their children.[69]

■ Quebec

The *Civil Code of Quebec* contains rules governing the rights and obligations of spouses (the primary regime) and also various matrimonial regimes, including partnership of acquests (the legal regime). The primary regime applies without exception to all spouses in Quebec, regardless of their matrimonial regime, the date of their marriage, or the provisions of any marriage contract between them.[70] It asserts the equality of the spouses, who together assume the moral and material direction of the family, and contribute toward the expenses of the marriage in proportion to their respective means, taking into account their respective responsibilities in the home.[71] There are also special provisions to protect the family residence and to remedy any unfairness that might result from a strict application of the matrimonial regime.[72]

Partnership of acquests governs all couples married after July 1, 1970, unless otherwise stipulated in a marriage contract.[73] Under the regime of partnership of acquests, the property of each spouse is divided into two groups: private property and acquests. The private property of a spouse consists of property owned by the spouse before the marriage; gifts and property acquired by inheritance since the marriage, and property acquired to replace private property; personal effects; instruments required for his or her occupation; diplomas; and so on.[74] Acquests include all other property, including the fruits and income due or collected from all private property or acquests during the regime.[75]

During the marriage, each spouse is entitled to administer his or her own private property and acquests, subject to specific rules governing the family residence and *inter vivos* gifts of acquests.[76] In the event that the matrimonial regime is dissolved, each spouse retains his or her private property and the acquests of each may be divided into two equal shares, if the spouses so choose.[77]

The other best-known regimes are community of property and separation as to property. All property of the spouses, with the exception of real property owned before the marriage or inherited from their ascendants during marriage, is covered under community of property.[78] In separation as to property, on the other hand, each spouse retains his or her independent patrimony.

Space limitations herein do not permit detailing of specific provisions for dissolution of the regime due to the death of a spouse. It is simply noted that, in certain circumstances, a spouse must choose between her share in the estate and in the matrimonial regime.[79] When a regime is dissolved for another reason, a woman in the home, for example, will retain half of her acquests (if any), and will receive half of the acquests of her husband; or she will be given half of the community property; or she will keep her property while he keeps his. "But that leaves her with nothing," one might say. Certainly, some matrimonial regimes, particularly separation as to property, will have inequitable results. This is precisely the reason for the existence of the special provision known as compensatory allowance.[80]

Compensatory allowance is intended to compensate for the contribution in goods or services by one of the spouses to the enrichment of the patrimony of the other, taking into consideration the marriage contract or matrimonial regime that applies to the situation.[81] An allowance may be in the form of a lump-sum payment, in cash or in instalments, or of a right of use, habitation, or even ownership of the family residence, depending on the circumstances. Case law is still unclear, not to say contradictory, as to the conditions under which this remedy may be allowed.[82] However, it appears that at the very least one must prove the following: contribution; enrichment of the patrimony of the other spouse, which continues to the time of the application; a causal relationship between the contribution and the enrichment; and the proportion of the enrichment attributable to the contribution.[83]

What constitutes a contribution? A contribution may be through services or property. Financial contribution for the purpose of acquisition of property by the other spouse is clearly a direct and immediate contribution. Contribution in services to a spouse's enterprise is also a contribution. This is why a spouse who raised eight children and also contributed to her husband's farm operation by working in the fields and tending to the animals was awarded a compensatory allowance of $25,000.[84] What about activities in the home? Here the situation remains uncertain. Some judges see such activities simply as a contribution to household responsibilities: a woman in the home is merely fulfilling her legal obligations. Moreover it is next to impossible to prove a cause-and-effect relationship between this kind of contribution and some form of enrichment of the spouse's patrimony.[85] On the other hand, however, some judges have emphasized the element of *enrichment* without requiring a direct relationship between the contribution and the enrichment.[86]

The conclusion to be drawn from all this is that the situation remains problematic. Compensatory allowance is a remedy in which judicial discretion will always play a large role. No one should count on this exceptional, after-the-fact remedy to ensure that her work is recognized: that would be to take one's future on the roll of the dice!

It bears repeating that, in essence, the matrimonial regime is a matter of choice. It is up to the spouses to decide what their financial relationship will be, and how their property may eventually be divided. In Quebec, the partnership of acquests, the legal regime since 1970, strikes a fine balance between independent management and division of property: a woman in the home is protected. However, a few striking statistics should be noted. In 1976, 56.87% of couples chose separation as to

property; in 1982, this figure fell to 42%.[87] For co-worker wives, there was
an opposite trend: in 1975, 54.6% were married but separate as to
property, compared to 59.9% in 1984.[88] Among farm women, the
situation was even more disheartening: 56.8% of married respondents
aged 20 to 24 in 1981 were separate as to property.[89] In total, 24.7% were
under community of property, 58% were separate as to property, and
10.2% were under partnership of acquests.[90] It seems that most notaries
recommend this regime for couples in business in order to protect some of
the woman's property in the event that the enterprise goes bankrupt.[91]
However, if the woman does not own any property, then she has nothing
to protect, and separation as to property offers, at best, an illusion of
security. The woman starts out poor, and stays poor!

Gifts and Inheritances

Transmission by gift or inheritance is another means of gaining access to
income or property. It is still rare for a woman to receive a farm operation
as a gift or inheritance from her father or her spouse. The patrilinear
tradition still prevails: land is handed down from father to son. The
difference in the ways in which land is passed on tends, rather, to reflect
the legal form of the enterprise: partnership interests or shares, as the
case may be. An exhaustive analysis of the ways in which ownership of
land is conveyed is clearly outside the scope of this study.

Nevertheless, by way of illustration, reference is made to a study
done in Quebec, designed to determine the problems facing farm families
and to explore new ways of conveying ownership of farms. In that study,
Lise Pilon-Lê found that three distinct methods of conveying ownership
had appeared in historical sequence: gift *inter vivos* (father to son); sale
by father to son (with a partial gift, consisting of the difference between
the sale price and the real market value of the farm); and new ways of
conveying ownership: the father-son partnership and the company.[92] The
most striking finding about these developments in the patrilinear
process is the constant and systematic exclusion of women from
ownership of land, first by their fathers and then by their husbands.[93]
And the tradition is still with us: girls get the furniture, and boys inherit
the land,[94] although some young women are beginning to challenge this
practice.

With the exception of this tradition, however, there is no legal
obstacle to farm women obtaining rights of ownership through gifts *inter*

vivos, testamentary legacies, or intestate succession. The only peculiarity that merits brief mention in this context is the interconnection between the matrimonial regime and intestate succession. For the purpose of illustration, the same three provinces are again considered.

■ Saskatchewan

In the event of the death of a spouse, the *Matrimonial Property Act* applies along with earlier legislation, namely the *Intestate Succession Act*,[95] the *Homestead Act*, and the *Dependants' Relief Act*. The *Intestate Succession Act* provides that when a spouse dies without a will and leaves an estate of less than $40,000 or has no issue, the surviving spouse is entitled to the entire estate.[96] The estate includes all real and personal property of the deceased, regardless of the use made of it.[97]

The surviving spouse must, within six months of the death, file an application for his or her share of the household property, which is "frozen" once the application is filed.[98] Any agreement or settlement respecting the matrimonial property has effect only by order of the court.[99] Property given to the survivor is deemed never to have been part of the estate of the deceased, and so does not fall into the estate and is not subject to the terms of the will.[100]

■ Ontario

The surviving spouse must choose between the rights under family property legislation and rights to the estate.[101] The *Succession Law Reform Act*[102] provides for an automatic reserve of $75,000, which goes first to the surviving spouse,[103] so that, if the value of the estate is less than $75,000, the surviving spouse is entitled to the entire estate.[104] If the deceased bequeaths part of his or her estate and dies intestate as to the remainder, the surviving spouse receives property with a minimum value of $75,000, even if the will provides for a lesser amount. On the other hand, if the will provides for a legacy of more than $75,000, the will applies. If no choice is made within six months following the death, the surviving spouse receives the share provided by succession legislation[105] rather than under family property legislation.

■ Quebec

When a spouse dies intestate, the surviving spouse must choose between his or her share under the matrimonial regime, and the share under the devolution of estates provisions.[106] In the absence of close family members, the surviving spouse will clearly be able to combine the rights under the matrimonial regime with rights to the estate. Close family members consist of children, father and mother, or collateral relations up to nephews and nieces in the first degree inclusively.[107]

When Bill 20 is enacted (an Act to add the reformed law of persons, successions, and property to the Civil Code of Quebec), it will amend the law that is now in effect in Quebec. Section 718 of the Bill provides that "the surviving spouse's heirship is not dependent on the renunciation of his matrimonial rights and benefits." The surviving spouse will therefore no longer have to make a choice, and may benefit from both the rights under his or her matrimonial regime and the rights to the estate.

OBSTACLES TO LEGAL AND ECONOMIC RECOGNITION

Credit

There are clear patterns in the relationships between farm women and lending institutions. First, the difficulties that farm women experience in obtaining credit, and secondly, the pressure exerted on them to personally guarantee any debt contracted by their husbands (thereby giving up any benefit that might accrue to them under the applicable matrimonial regime), are concrete manifestations of the growing debt that burdens the family enterprise and that characterizes modern farming.

■ Difficulties in Obtaining Credit

In 1970, a report by the Royal Commission on the Status of Women in Canada stated: "It was made clear in briefs and letters to the Commission that women are not granted credit as freely as men."[108]

In 1980, the situation was scarcely any better. A study conducted in Montreal[109] found that many loan officers exhibited a discriminatory attitude toward women. It was observed that subjective factors and personal feelings of the loan officers influenced their attitudes and criteria in lending money.[110]

Also, the Ontario Ministry of Agriculture states that 47 per cent of women in rural communities classify obtaining credit among the ten most important problems to be solved.[111] Farm women complain especially of the discriminatory attitude encountered when they apply for credit, or when they want to have their own credit history recognized.[112]

These women have legitimate grievances. Legislation providing access to credit, including farm credit, generally provides that legal or common-law spouses operating farms are to be considered as one person, while two other people, even if they are partners, and even if they are father and son, two brothers or two sisters, are considered as separate entities and are both entitled to the benefits of the legislation. Other statutes, such as the *Prairie Grain Advance Payments Act*,[113] have been amended to remedy this problem and recognize partnerships between spouses.[114] In Quebec, clear progress has been made as a result of the *Act to Promote the Development of Agriculture Operations* enacted on June 19, 1986. This new legislation provides that the start-up grant for new agricultural producers will rise from $8,000 to $15,000; the discriminatory clause that put married couples at a disadvantage has been repealed.[115]

In 1980, application forms for farm credit were often addressed solely to men, thus minimizing the contributions of women to farming.[116] Some forms were also discriminatory in that they required information on the number of male children on the farm, and disregarded daughters.[117]

But there has been some change, reflected by the activities of the Société du crédit agricole, which was set up in order to assist farmers having difficulties, as well as aspiring farmers, in maintaining and starting up profitable farm operations. The eligibility criteria are simple: an applicant must be of the required legal age to obtain a mortgage, must be a Canadian citizen or permanent resident, and must demonstrate that the income from the enterprise, together with all his or her supplementary income, will be sufficient to meet all financial obligations and to ensure a suitable standard of living.

The application forms used by the Société no longer contain questions that are in themselves discriminatory; nonetheless the fact remains that very few women obtain credit. If the large sums of money needed for a farm operation are to be obtained, property must be provided as security for repayment of the loan or, at the very least, the borrower must have a regular income. Since farm women generally have neither income nor property, a vicious circle is created.

■ Guarantees

The requirement of guarantees poses a major problem for farm women today. Most financial institutions require, as a condition of obtaining a loan, that the wife personally guarantee the debt, even if the husband is the sole owner of the farm.[118] Thus, a married woman separate as to property, with paid employment outside the home, may be asked to repay, out of her own salary, a debt that was taken out in the interest of her husband alone. On the other hand, a wife who used her salary to pay for the groceries and the children's clothing will not be considered by the courts as having contributed to the farm operation as such.

But how can a farm woman refuse to sign, when the bank is threatening to demand immediate repayment of all loans and bring on the inevitable bankruptcy of the farm enterprise? Or, as one farm woman from Kemptville, Ontario said: "How can I refuse the guarantee, when we need the money to buy seed, and we have to seed next week? We don't have time to shop around, to go from one village to the next looking for another bank that will give us a loan without my guarantee!" The Comité des femmes en agriculture de Lanaudière (Quebec) made similar comments: it wants to end the present practice whereby a loan officer requires the wife's personal property as security for the husband's loan. Loan officers should require security that is proportionate to, and not worth more than, the amount borrowed, and the family home should not be required as security.[119]

One might doubt the legal validity of these extorted guarantees. In an Ontario case, a bank had required that a wife sign a guarantee at a time when the husband was seriously indebted, without informing the wife of the extent of the indebtedness. The court declared the guarantee invalid, because the bank had not provided the wife with the information to which she was entitled.[120] Some financial institutions require that the wife obtain independent legal advice from a lawyer or notary and that she acknowledge in the guarantee document itself that she has indeed received legal advice and understood its significance.[121] It is also uncertain whether a bank may act on its threat without exposing itself to an action for damages.[122]

What advice should be given to these women? Obviously, *don't sign*. But if it is necessary to sign, at the very least be sure that an equivalent right of ownership is obtained; don't agree to repay a mortgage if you are not the owner of the property involved; plan financial needs so that time is available to negotiate with various financial institutions; combine efforts with neighbours and make sure that everyone refuses to sign. Or, if it is necessary to sign, guarantee only a specific amount[123] and arrange to have the guarantee lifted once the debt is repaid. These options can only be referred to as making the best of a bad situation.

Tradition and Bonds of Affection

Even today, the law offers a variety of possibilities to a farm woman seeking recognition of her work. However, all these choices may create their own problems for women who can rarely take time out to plan their lives. This, of course, is a question of self-perception, as well as of how one perceives others.

Problems in obtaining credit, and the requirement of personal guarantees, are evidence of a discriminatory attitude toward women. As already pointed out, farm women face extreme prejudices, often because of the traditional communities in which they are seeking change. Attitudes in rural communities change slowly, as they do everywhere, particularly because people in authority are being asked not only to change their behaviour, but also to see with new eyes what has always been there and, finally, to admit that women's work is indeed work and, ultimately, that women are independent people and not extensions of their husbands.

If farm women today are not making full use of existing legal structures enabling them to obtain complete legal and economic recognition and the power that such recognition would bring with it, it is certainly because of tradition and a lack of information; but it is also because there are not enough people in the professional community who are capable of taking an interest in their problems and who are prepared to answer their questions. In this regard, an interesting initiative has been taken by the Quebec ministère de l'Agriculture, des Pêcheries et de l'Alimentation, which on January 29, 1986 launched a three-year plan of action for farm women entitled, "From Sharing the Work to Sharing the Power." The ministry intends, in this way, to encourage recognition of farm women by providing them with access to ownership, income, benefits, and membership in regional farm women's committees. It hopes to do this through "financial assistance to the Comité provincial and to regional farm women committees, and through the professional and technical support provided by the Bureau de la répondante à la condition féminine."[124] Such government action is intended mainly to provide training and information to encourage farm women to take charge of their own futures.

However, apart from the present economic crisis and the financial pressures on farm enterprises, the biggest problem facing farm women seeking immediate financial independence is undeniably the difficulty of negotiating with their husbands. Anyone who wants change must be able to show that it is beneficial, if not essential. Stacked against the change a woman seeks is all the force of inertia and tradition. Any change that upsets not only everyday life but also the perception of authority relationships and self-esteem is an even greater threat. In any discussion between spouses, there is an emotional overlay that may strengthen one's natural resistance to change. In extreme cases, independence may come only with the breakdown of the relationship.

In view of all these obstacles, what sort of future can farm women look forward to? If the ultimate objective is full legal and financial recognition of the contribution of women in agriculture, must a woman direct her efforts toward creating new legal structures through legislative amendments, or must she speed up changes in attitude by using currently available opportunities to the fullest extent possible? To deal with this question, a brief analysis of the status of *co-worker* as a model for new structures follows, after which the various desired changes in attitude are discussed. Finally a plan of action is formulated.

A New Structure: Proposal for a Declaration of Status[125]

In Quebec, the Association des femmes collaboratrices (ADFC) is seeking enactment of a model statute for family enterprises, including farm enterprises, which would be administered by the ministère des Institutions financières. Its primary aim would be to provide recognition in commercial law for work performed by the co-worker spouse, by offering a choice between two possible legal statuses: spouse-employee and co-worker spouse.

The choice of *employee* status would entitle the spouse to a salary based on the duties performed and the usual benefits to which an employee would be entitled, such as minimum wage, paid vacation, unemployment insurance, maternity leave, opportunities for professional training or for retraining, compensation for accidents on the job, and participation in the Régime de rentes du Québec. In addition, the employee could personally benefit from certain income tax deductions, such as those for child care, registered retirement savings plan contributions, and so on.[126] He or she would be entitled to professional recognition and to the benefits that such recognition brings. In the event that the enterprise, employment, or cohabitation cease, he or she would be entitled to receive severance pay and confirmation of employment, as well as to claim unpaid wages in the event of a bankruptcy.

On the other hand, the status of *co-worker* would entitle the spouse to the usual benefits of partnership: a right to draw from accounts and to receive benefits and professional recognition on the same footing as the other spouse. During the joint operation of the enterprise, there would be two distinct sets of assets: the property forming part of the *family enterprise*, and the matrimonial property as determined under the matrimonial property regime in each case. Termination of the enterprise would result in a 50-50 division of the net assets belonging to the owner and forming part of the enterprise; termination of cohabitation would have the added result of a division of the matrimonial property according to the usual rules. In the event of the death of one spouse, the co-worker spouse would be entitled to continue operating the enterprise. In the event of divorce or separation, judgement could be obtained ordering the forced withdrawal of the co-worker spouse.

In order to exercise one's choice and to obtain one status or the other, it would be sufficient for the couple or the co-worker spouse (defined as the spouse who is not the owner of the enterprise) to register a declaration of family enterprise, setting out the choice of status, in the index of family enterprises, which would be specially created for this purpose. The term *spouse* would also include common-law spouses who had cohabited for at least three years, and *family enterprise* would be defined as any project of a financial nature in which a couple participates.

Legal writers have analysed the strictly legal problems of this proposal, particularly in view of its coercive nature and the administrative burdens and complexities it would involve.[127] However, a thorough analysis of these difficulties is outside the scope of this study. It is noted that the concept of voluntary declaration of status put forward by the ADFC is intended to equalize the power relationship between spouses by adding the weight of the state behind the weaker side, usually the woman. This is a measure designed to prompt, if not to coerce, a recalcitrant spouse, if he creates obstacles intended to hinder his wife from becoming a partner or shareholder-director. It is probably true, however, that a farm woman who is hesitant to open negotiations, or who has been presented with a categorical refusal, will be as fearful, if not more so, to register a declaration of status and to set the administrative machine in motion.[128] The isolation of the farm woman makes her particularly vulnerable to fear of reprisals, whether or not such fear is justified. This is why the efforts of the ADFC as well as thorough discussion within farm women's groups are crucial at this stage. Such initiatives are useful in developing solutions appropriate to the daily realities of farm women's lives, and help to ensure that farm women have security and financial independence.

In 1985, in response to the proposals of the ADFC, the government created a task force that formulated a series of recommendations on methods of recognizing status. The government of Quebec then undertook to act on these recommendations, beginning in the fall of 1986.[129]

New Attitudes

Recognition of the work of farm women will require new attitudes toward their status as producers, on the part of both the community and farm women themselves. The community must be considered to include financial and legal institutions and the professionals working in them (loan officers, legal advisers, judges), as well as the family environment (spouse and children). What is meant by *contribution* and *work* must be redefined.

Farm women must also encourage such awareness, and equip themselves for this process. Among the informational tools they will need, particular reference is made to legal material directed specifically at young women, to inform them of the choices they must make when they marry and the different consequences that flow from each of these choices.

Farm women should also consider adapting techniques developed by unions for use in asserting their collective power against financial institutions that demand personal guarantees, or against legal advisers who fail to explain the consequences of signing such guarantees.

At the political level, support and encouragement should be given to groups of farm women hoping to "save the family farm," to preserve the quality of life in rural communities, and to promote the special position of women in their communities.

A Plan of Action

First, information is needed. All members of the professional community should be required to provide clear information and a range of options for recognizing the contribution of farm women. Once the structure is selected, it is of prime importance that a farm woman arm herself with legal evidence of her work and her investments in the farm. It may be necessary to change the matrimonial property regime, in jurisdictions where that is permitted, in order to provide better recognition of work done both in the home and within the farm operation. It is essential that a record of her contributions in time and money be kept. The constant goals must be to obtain credit and ownership rights, and to formalize the partnership within the family enterprise.

The current situation should then be put in order by preparing oneself to negotiate within the family, without being swayed by arguments about the cost ("It's too expensive to change the matrimonial regime." "Notaries' fees are exhorbitant, just for putting your name on a title.")

The pioneering work done by the Association des femmes collaboratrices and other groups helping women to become aware of the value of their work and of how to have it recognized is of fundamental importance in the women's movement in Canada. Women must, all together, undertake a personal analysis of their perceptions of money. As Suzanne Dion put it:

> I suspect that here women are victims of their problems in relating to money. Even women who are good administrators find it difficult to take money or property for themselves. It is as if money were dirty, as if a woman should not want too much money . . . [130]

Farm women are not unique. We all have problems in seeing money as a tool to be used to ultimately give us access to independence and power.

Power is another threatening word for many women. Powerless as women have been for so long, they are almost as afraid of it as they are of money and the desire for money. Here, the enormous differences between women's and men's values come to the forefront.[131] Need it be said that our legal system reflects men's values? To paraphrase Germaine Greer, the problem is not that most judges are men, but that the law is male.[132]

What about time? The leitmotiv weaving through all the conversations, discussions, studies, and analyses of women is the little time women have in their daily lives to perform their many roles and duties. As Suzanne Dion noted, farm women's lack of time covers a more fundamental problem: the need to redefine their roles and to find ways of organizing their lives.[133]

Perhaps the solution lies in another direction. Women could repossess their time, take it for themselves, keep it, use it, waste it, or structure it differently. Gloria Steinem said that women's sense of time, their capacity to make long-term plans, is a function of their real or perceived power.[134] Women must stop living by reacting, from crisis to crisis, without taking initiatives or making personal plans. Taking time out gives them a chance to change course.[135]

But apart from personal initiatives, banking institutions, planners, and decision-makers must make more room for women in policies that directly concern women or that affect the farm industry as a whole. In short, farm women must not only penetrate those sectors where their contributions are still hidden or unrecognized as essential to the operation of Canadian farm, they must also transform them.

80 **NOTES**

**Farm women:
Obtaining legal
and economic
recognition of
their work**

1. In the 1981 Quebec study by
   Suzanne Dion, 95% of the
   respondents were married, and
   89% had children. Suzanne Dion,
   *Les Femmes dans l'agriculture au
   Québec* (Longueuil, Quebec: Les
   éditions La Terre de chez nous,
   1983), p. 24. Another study by
   Women for the Survival of
   Agriculture in eastern Ontario in
   1985 found that 96% of farm
   women were married (Women for
   the Survival of Agriculture, *What
   Are You Worth? A Study of the
   Economic Contribution of Eastern
   Ontario Farm Women to the
   Family Farm Enterprise*, study
   presented at the Second National
   Farm Women's Conference,
   Charlottetown, Prince Edward
   Island, November 21-24, 1985, p.
   5).

2. In Quebec, 78% of respondents had
   another occupation before working
   in agriculture, and 15% (25% of
   respondents aged 20 to 25) had
   maintained employment outside
   the farm enterprise (Dion, *Les
   femmes dans l'agriculture au
   Quebec*, p. 34). In eastern Ontario,
   30% of farm women work
   elsewhere: 20% full-time and 10%
   part-time (Women for the Survival
   of Agriculture, *What Are You
   Worth?*, p. 6).

3. In Quebec, more than a third of
   respondents work more than 30
   hours per week in the spring (35%),
   the fall (36%), and the summer
   (56%) (Dion, *Les femmes dans
   l'agriculture au Québec*, p. 39). A
   1981 study by the National
   Farmers Union indicated that farm
   women in Canada devote an
   average of 28 hours per week to
   farm work, and that 79% of them
   were not paid (Women for the
   Survival of Agriculture, *What Are
   You Worth?*, p. 10-11).

4. It is interesting (and disturbing) to
   note that, in Quebec, 42% of farm
   women have invested funds in the
   farm enterprise (salary, savings
   prior to marriage or inheritance),
   but only 21% are owners,
   shareholders, or partners (Dion,
   *Les femmes dans l'agriculture au
   Québec*, p. 38). In eastern Ontario,
   farm women also contributed
   capital for the purchase of land
   (43%), buildings (36%), livestock
   (34%), and equipment (43%); 79%
   had these contributions legally
   recognized in the case of land; 65%
   in the case of buildings; but only
   54% in the case of livestock and
   55% in the case of equipment
   (Women for the Survival of
   Agriculture, *What Are You
   Worth?*, p. 7).

5. In Quebec, 3.5% of respondents
   were sole proprietors; 17.7%
   shareholders or partners; 5.3%
   employees; 73.2% co-worker wives;
   and 0.3% retired (Dion, *Les
   femmes dans l'agriculture au
   Québec*, p. 35). In eastern Ontario,
   only 4% of respondents were sole
   proprietors; 69% were co-owners
   with their husbands (Women for
   the Survival of Agriculture, *What
   Are You Worth?*, p. 4). A study of
   farm women in Prince Edward
   Island showed that 73% took part
   in farm work, but only 11% were
   paid (Women for the Survival of
   Agriculture, *What Are You
   Worth?*, p. 15). A word of caution: it

is difficult to estimate the validity of this data, since many farm women state that they are co-owners or co-workers because of the work they do and their own personal approach to it, without being able to provide any legally acceptable documentation of their claim.

6. Dion, *Les femmes dans l'agriculture au Québec*, p. 45.

7. In a study done in Ontario, for example, respondents assessed their own contribution as 22% of the farm work; however, a thorough analysis showed that they are responsible for 47% of farm work and 97% of the child-care and housekeeping duties; this includes the 68% of farm women who regularly attend to the personal needs of employees (washing, cooking, housekeeping) and the 22% who sometimes perform this extra work (Women for the Survival of Agriculture, *What Are You Worth?*, p. 8). The author adds: "Few women realize however, that 'chatting' with sales people is really doing the work of a purchasing agent.'" (*What Are You Worth?*, p. 7). For an example of farm women's systematic undervaluation of their work, see: *What Are You Worth?*, pp. 12-13. See also: Micheline Desjardins, *On ne compte pas! Dossier socio-économique sur la situation des femmes collaboratrices dans les Prairies* (Ottawa: Fédération des femmes canadiennes-françaises, 1984), p. 24. The government of Alberta, which is aware of the problem, has published a pamphlet to assist farm women in recording their hours of work by category (e.g., care of animals, management, bookkeeping, maintenance), in order to assess their own economic contribution (Alberta Agriculture, Home Economics Branch, *Partners in Agriculture: The Farm Wife's Economic Contribution to the Agricultural Business* (Edmonton: Alberta, 1983), Homedex 1830-11). Micheline Desjardins (*On ne compte pas!*, pp.29-30) also proposed a more rudimentary exercise for co-worker wives to do in order to keep track of the time devoted to housekeeping work and activities in the family business.

8. Canada, Royal Commission of Inquiry on the Status of Women in Canada, *Report* (Ottawa: Information Canada, 1970).

9. On this point, see: Canada, Statistics Canada, *Women in Canada: A Statistical Report* (Ottawa: Supply and Services Canada, 1985), catalogue no. 89-503E, p. xiv.
   • in 1982, women's average earnings were 64% of those of men; this figure is up from 60% in 1971;
   • families headed by women aged 15-64 have incomes which average half those of families headed by men;
   • in 1982, 45% of families headed by women aged 15-64 and 60% of unattached elderly women had incomes below Statistics Canada's Low-Income Cut-Offs;
   • since the mid-1970s, violent crimes against women have increased at a faster rate than most other types of violent crimes.

10. *Murdoch* v. *Murdoch*, (1975), 1 S.C.R. 423.

11. For example, there are the Association féminine d'éducation

et d'action sociale (AFEAS), the
Association des femmes
collaboratrices (ADFC), the
recently formed Comité des
femmes en Agriculture of the
Unions des producteurs agricoles
(UPA), Women in Support of
Agriculture (Prince Edward Island
and Ontario), Women for the
Survival of Agriculture and
Concerned Farm Women (Ontario),
and Women of Unifarm (Alberta)
— as well as the women's wing of
the National Farmers Union, and
many others.

12. Studies presented at the First
National Farm Women's
Conference, held in Ottawa in
December 1980.

13. Suzanne Dion, "The Effects of the
Agricultural Crisis on the Farm
Woman's Family and Her Rural
Community," paper presented at
the Second National Farm
Women's Conference,
Charlottetown, Prince Edward
Island, November 21-24, 1985, p. 3.

14. See, for example: Association
féminine d'éducation et d'action
sociale (AFEAS), "The Wife
Contributing with her Husband to
an Enterprise for Profit: Revised
Recommendations, September
1979," *First National Farm
Women's Conference Background
Papers*, Ottawa, December 2-4,
1980.

15. *Civil Code of Quebec*, Arts. 464
and 480 to 517, and Arts. 458, 459,
and 559 (S.Q. 1980, c. 39); *Family
Law Reform Act*, R.S.O. 1980, c.
152, as amended by the *Act to
Amend the Family Law Reform
Act*; the *Matrimonial Property Act*,
R.S.A. 1980, c. M-9; *The Family
Relations Act*, R.S.B.C. 1979, c.
121; *The Matrimonial Property*

Act, S.N.B. 1980, c. M-11, as
amended by S.N.B. 1980, c. 24, s.
11; *The Matrimonial Property Act*,
S. Nfld. 1979, c. 32; *Family Law
Reform Act*, S.P.E.I. 1978, c. 6; The
Marital Property Act, S.M. 1978, c.
24 (also C.C.S.M., c. M45); 1983
R.S.M., c. 53; The *Matrimonial
Property Act*, S.S. 1979, c. M-6.1;
Matrimonial Property Act, S.N.S.
1980, c. 9. On this point generally,
see: Freda M. Steel, "The Ideal
Marital Property Regime: What
Would It Be?" in *Family Law in
Canada: New Directions* (Ottawa:
Canadian Advisory Council on the
Status of Women, 1985), pp.
127-168, and particularly p. 130 et
seq.

16. Subsections 74(3) and 74(4) of the
Income Tax Act, S.C. 1970-71-72, c.
63, repealed by S.C. 1980-81, c. 48,
subs. 40(1), which applies to
remuneration paid after 1979 for
services rendered as an employee
after 1979. Sections 457 and 458 of
the *Quebec Taxation Act*, R.S.Q., c.
I-3, repealed in March 1980.

17. Subsection 74(5) of the *Income Tax
Act*, repealed by S.C. 1980-81, c.
48, subs. 40(1), which applies to
fiscal years ending after December
11, 1979. Section 465 of the *Quebec
Taxation Act*, repealed in March
1980. The salary or shares thus
paid or given to a co-worker spouse
are also exempt from the normal
operation of the rules for
attribution of income, by virtue of
which the income from property
(including a salary) transferred to a
spouse is taxable in the hands of
the transferor subs. 74(6) *Income
Tax Act*, s. 456 *Quebec Taxation
Act*.

18. The Canada Pension Plan and the
Régime des rentes du Québec were

amended to permit the division of pension credits accumulated by a spouse during the marriage, on request, at the time of divorce. S. 53.2 of the *Canada Pension Plan*, R.S.C. 1970, c. C-5, added by S.C. 1976-77, c. 36, s. 7; ss. 102.1 to 102.5 of the *Act respecting the Régime des rentes du Québec*, R.S.Q., c. R-9, added on June 1, 1979. Louise Dulude found that only 3% of former spouses who were eligible for such a division had taken advantage of their right (Louise Dulude, *Love, Marriage and Money... An Analysis of Financial Relations Between the Spouses* (Ottawa: Canadian Advisory Council on the Status of Women, 1984,) p. 41).

19. In legal terms this is a divorce based on marriage breakdown. *Divorce Act, 1985*, enacted by the House of Commons on January 23, 1986.

20. *Family Orders and Agreements Enforcement Assistance Act*, enacted by the House of Commons on January 23, 1986.

21. The Quebec *Labour Code*, R.S.Q., c. C-27, subs. 1(1).

22. See, for example, the definition of "employee" in the *Labour Standards Act*, R.S.Q., c. N-1.1, s. 1, which reads as follows:

"employee" means a person who works *for* an employer and who is entitled to a wage; this word also includes a worker who is a party to a contract, under which he:

i. undertakes to perform specified work for a person *within the scope and in accordance with the methods and means determined by that person*;

ii. undertakes to furnish, for the carrying out of the contract, the material, equipment, raw materials or merchandise chosen by that person and *to use them in the manner indicated by him*;...

(emphasis added.)

23. For example, s. 93 of the Quebec *Labour Standards Act* states that the provisions of that act are matters of public order, that is, that any derogation, even by the mutual consent of the parties, is void by law. Similar provisions are found in the statutes of the common law provinces.

24. Quebec *Labour Standards Act*, ss. 40 et seq.

25. Quebec *Labour Standards Act*, ss. 60 et seq.

26. Quebec *Labour Standards Act*, ss. 122 et seq.

27. Section 63 *Income Tax Act*, ss. 351 to 356 *Quebec Taxation Act*.

28. Paragraphs 60(i) and 146(1)(c) *Income Tax Act*, para. 339(b) and s. 925 *Quebec Taxation Act*.

29. For example, the following jobs do not provide pension eligibility (for Canada Pension Plan purposes):

(2) Excepted employment is

(a) Employment in agriculture or an agricultural enterprise, horticulture, fishing, hunting, trapping, forestry, logging or lumbering by an employer who either pays the employee less than $250 in cash remuneration in a year or employs the employee, on terms providing for payment of cash remuneration, for a period of less than 25 working days in a year; . . .

(Canada Pension Plan, R.S.C. 1970, c. C-5, subs. 6(2), as amended by 1974-75-76, c. 4, s. 2; 1980-81-82-83, c. 48, s. 121).

30. By virtue of the *Unemployment Insurance Act, 1971*, S.C. 1970-71-72, c. 48, certain employments are not insurable within the terms of the Act, particularly employment of a person by his or her spouse. In addition, paragraph 14(a) of the *Unemployment Insurance Regulations* adds:
The following employments are excepted from insurable employment:
(a) employment of a person by a corporation if he or his spouse, individually or in combination, controls more than 40 per cent of the voting shares of that corporation;
. . .
employment of a person if he is not paid any of his remuneration in cash; . . .
(Unemployment Insurance, C.R.C. 1978, c. 1576, as amended by SOR/78-710, s. 1).

31. In Quebec, a co-worker wife may rely on the Quebec *Labour Standards Act* to obtain a salary, but a farm woman who is an employee employed for the operation of a farm operated by her husband with the habitual assistance of not more than three employees is expressly excluded from the scope of the Act (s. 3).

32. Ruth Rose-Lizée, *Portrait des femmes collaboratrices du Québec* (Saint-Lambert: Association des femmes collaboratrices du Québec), 1984, p. 95. See also Pamela Smith's article in this publication.

33. Rose-Lizée, *Portrait de femmes collaboratrices du Québec*, p. 97.

34. *Ibid.*, p. 99.

35. *Ibid.*, p. 97.

36. *Ibid.*

37. Farm woman quoted by Dion, *Les femmes dans l'agriculture du Québec*, p. 81.

38. (1984), 1 S.C.R. 2, reversing (1982) C.A. 66, reversing (1979) C.S.

39. (1984), 1 S.C.R. 2, reversing (1982), C.A. 66, reversing (1979) C.S. 407.

40. (1984), 1 S.C.R. 2, reversing (1982), C.A. 75.

41. (1984), 1 S.C.R. 2, reversing (1982), C.A. 75, p. 12.

. . . The appellate judges were of the view that plaintiff was not able to discharge the burdent of proof placed upon her. This I feel is understandable, for I consider, as did Paré J.A., that a refusal by appellant to be a party to the purchase of the farm would be crucial in determining whether the latter was done as part of a partnership, and such a refusal is a significant factor in identifying the *affectio societatis* which should exist between the partners. (p. 12)

42. The term "corporation" refers to any legal person, that is, any person created by law. The term "company" is reserved to commercial corporations, as opposed to municipal, Crown, or non-profit corporations.

In Canada, there is dual jurisdiction over incorporations, so that the provinces have exclusive power over corporations with provincial objects, while the federal government has power over any other corporations by virtue of the residual power. SS. 91 and 92 of the *Constitution Act, 1867*. The powers of a company are determined by its constitution, its by-laws (or letters patent, as the case may be), and by other federal or provincial statutes.

43. For example, the right of dissent contained in s. 194 of the *Canada Business Corporations Act* and the remedy provided in s. 234 of the Act.

44. Analysis of the hidden nature of domestic work and the contribution of women is outside the scope of this study. Interested readers are advised to read Louise Vandelac et al., *Du travail et de l'amour: les dessous de la production domestique* (Montreal: Albert Saint-Martin, 1985). See also: Desjardins, *On ne compte pas!*, p. 8 et seq., in which the total annual cost in 1983 of replacing the domestic services provided by women was determined to be $13,151, not counting maintaining family relationships, visits to the dentist and doctor, and so on.

45. *Murdoch* v. *Murdoch* (1975) 1 S.C.R. 423.

46. See: Association féminine d'éducation et d'action sociale (AFEAS), "The Wife Contributing with her Husband to an Enterprise for Profit." See also: Dulude, *Love, Marriage and Money*...

47. Freda M. Steel, "The Ideal Marital Property Regime — What Would It Be?", p. 130 et seq.

48. S.S. 1979 (Sask.), c. M-6.1.

49. S.S. 1979, c. M-6.1, Section 20 of the Act reads:

    20. The purpose of this Act, and in particular of this Part (distribution of matrimonial property), is to recognize that child care, household management and

financial provision are the joint and mutual responsibilities of spouses and that inherent in the marital relationship there is joint contribution, whether financial or otherwise, by the spouses to the assumption of these responsibilities that entitles each spouse to an equal distribution of the marimonial property, subject to the exceptions, exemptions and equitable considerations mentioned in this Act.

50. S.S. 1979, c. M-6.1, s. 4.

51. S.S. 1979, c. M-6.1, s. 2(h) and s. 23.

52. S.S. 1979, c. M-6.1, s. 5 and s. 22. The spouse who alleges that an equal division of property would be inequitable has the burden of proof.

53. S.S. 1979, c. M-6.1, s. 21 and s. 22.

54. *Donkin v. Bugoy*, (1985) 2 S.C.R. 85, reversing (1981) 4 W.W.R. 136. At trial, the Court had considered these factors, and had refused to order division of the matrimonial home (the exclusive property of Mr. Bugoy) and had attributed to Mrs. Donkin's estate the amount of $10,000 out of property of the marriage having a total value of $132,000. This judgement was confirmed on appeal to the Saskatchewan Court of Appeal, without written reasons (p. 90).

55. R.S.S. 1978, c. H-5.

56. *Matrimonial Property Act*, ss. 9 and 22. See also *Donkin* v. *Bugoy*, and the cases cited therein.

57. *Matrimonial Property Act*, ss. 21 and 24. This was undoubtedly a reaction to the *Intestate Succession Act*, by virtue of which a wife who had left the home and was living in an adulterous

relationship lost her right to any
share in the estate (s. 18).

58. *Matrimonial Property Act*, s. 23.

59. *Matrimonial Property Act*,
Sections 25, 26 and 43.

60. R.S.O. 1980, c. 152.

61. *Family Law Act*, 1986, which
received royal assent on January
17, 1986, and came into force on
March 1, 1986, with retroactive
effect to June 4, 1985.

62. Section 5 of the *Family Law Act*
reads as follows:

    5(7) The purpose of this section is
    to recognize that child care,
    household management and
    financial provision are the joint
    responsibility of the spouses and
    that inherent in the marital
    relationship there is equal
    contribution, whether financial or
    otherwise, by the spouses to the
    assumption of these
    responsibilities, entitling each
    spouse to the equalization of the
    net family properties, subject only
    to the equitable consideration set
    out in subsection (6).

63. *Family Law Act*, Section 5; see also
the definition of the word
"property" and the expression "net
family property" in s. 4 of the Act.

64. *Family Law Act*, 1986, Section 18
et seq. It should be noted that only
that portion of the property
reasonably considered necessary to
the normal enjoyment of the
residence is considered to be the
matrimonial home.

65. *Family Law Act*, 1986, Section 9 et
seq.

66. *Family Law Act*, 1986, Subsection
5(6).

67. *Family Law Act*, 1986, Section 11.

68. *Family Law Act*, 1986, Section 51
et seq. Contrary to the situation in
Quebec, the spouses may even
agree on their support obligations,
Art. 440, *Civil Code of Quebec*.

69. *Family Law Act*, 1986, Section 53.
See also "paternity agreements," s.
59.

70. Articles 440 et seq., *Civil Code of
Quebec*, S.Q. 1980, c. 39, Art. 65.

71. *Civil Code of Quebec*, Articles 441,
443, 445.

72. *Civil Code of Quebec*, Articles 449
to 462.

73. *Civil Code of Quebec*, Articles 463
et seq.

74. *Civil Code of Quebec*, Article 482.

75. *Civil Code of Quebec*, Article 481.

76. *Civil Code of Quebec*, Articles 493
to 496.

77. *Civil Code of Quebec*, Articles 497
to 517.

78. *C.C.L.C.*, Article 1276. On this
point generally, see: E. Caparros,
*Les régimes matrimoniaux au
Québec* (Montreal: Wilson &
Lafleur, 1985), p. 199 et seq.

79. *C.C.L.C.*, Article 624c. On the
recommendation of the Office de
révision du Code Civil, this
provision will be repealed. Bill 20
contains no corresponding
provision.

80. *Civil Code of Quebec*, Articles 439,
459, 533, 559 and 735.1 *C.C.L.C.*

81. *Civil Code of Quebec*, Article 559.

82. See the summaries of recent cases
in: Richard Gaudreau, *Litiges entre
conjoints de droit et de fait*,
professional development course of
the Barreau du Québec
(Cowansville: Les Éditions Yvon

Blais, 1985-86), vol. 3, p. 175 et seq.

83. *Droit de la famille-176* (1985) C.A. 5 Turgeon, McCarthy and Tyndale J.J.

84. *Droit de la famille-166*, J.E. 84-861, S.C., Fraser Martin J.

85. *Droit de la famille-67* (1985) C.A. 135, per Nichols J., pp. 150-151.

86. *Droit de la famille-67* (1985) C.A. 135, per Vallerand J., at pp. 153-154; per Beauregard J. (dissenting in part), at p. 142.

87. Data provided by the Service des registres de régimes matrimoniaux, ministère de la Justice, Quebec City, cited by Monique Charlebois, "Quebec Family Property Law: In Need of Reform," in *Women, the Law and the Economy*, ed. Diane Pask, Kathleen E. Mahoney, and Catherine A. Brown (Toronto: Butterworths, 1985), p. 240.

88. Rose-Lizée, *Portrait des femmes collaboratrices du Québec*, p. 104.

89. Dion, *Les femmes dans l'agriculture au Québec*, p. 134.

90. *Ibid.*

91. Rose-Lizée, *Portrait des femmes collaboratrices de Québec*, p. 105.

92. Lise Pilon-Lê, "Logique productiviste contre logique paysanne: la transmission des fermes spécialisées au Québec," unpublished, p. 6. According to Pilon-Lê, the size of the farm appears to play a role: "sale from father to son occurs on farms having a value of less than $300,000 when one son alone takes over the farm; father-son partnerships occur on farms having a value of between $300,000 and $600,000, with a relatively young father and one or two interested sons; corporate structure is suitable for large farms having a value of over $600,000, in which two to four children become involved in the farm" *(translation)*, p. 14. Pilon-Lê also noted that "debts of two and a half times greater for farmers who have chosen partnerships or corporations than for those who sold the farm to a son" *(translation)*, p. 14.

93. Pilon-Lê, "Logique productiviste contre logique paysanne," p. 7.

94. *Ibid.*

95. R.S.S. 1978, c. I-13.

96. R.S.S., 1978, c. I-13, s. 18.

97. R.S.R., 1978, c. I-13, s. 2.

98. S.S. 1979, c. M-6.1, s. 30.

99. S.S. 1979, c. M-6.1, subs. 34(3).

100. S.S. 1979, c. M-6.1, s. 30.

101. *An Act to revise the Family Law Reform Act*, s. 6., R.S.O.

102. R.S.O. 1980, c. 488.

103. The term "spouse" is defined in s. 1 of the *Act to revise the Family Law Reform Act:*"

"spouse means either of a man and woman who;

(a) are married to each other; or

(b) have together entered into a marriage that is voidable or void, in good faith on the part of the person asserting a right under this Act.

104. *Act to revise the Family Law Reform Act*, s. 1. This section states that all real or personal property of the deceased is included in the estate, regardless of the use made of such property.

105. *Act to revise the Family Law Reform Act*, ss. 45 and 46.

106. Article 624c, *C.C.L.C.*

107. Article 624c, *C.C.L.C.*

108. Carol McLeod, "Shadow of the Eight Ball: Women and Credit in Canada," *Rights and Liberties*, Canadian Rights and Liberties Federation, vol. 56, p. 11 (summer 1985).

109. Study by Lawrence Kyzanowski and Elizabeth Bertin-Boussu, reported by Julie White, *Bank and Credit Policies* (Ottawa: Canadian Human Rights Commission, 1981), p. 12.

110. For example, level of education and marital and family status are among the personal factors that influence the attitude of loan officers to women and credit. As well, the responses to the questionnaire were seen to vary considerably within the same financial institution.

111. Molly McGhee, *Women in Rural Life, the Changing Scene* (Toronto: Ministry of Agriculture and Food, 1981).

112. A concrete example of this situation: Chris Banman operated a dairy farm with her husband in Saskatchewan; she handled all the business transactions, the administration, and the bookkeeping for the farm operation; "But when they negotiated a loan in the early stages of the 10-year-old operation, only her husband's statements about the business were considered credible, even though he had to refer to her throughout the interview for answers to the questions." Liz Delahey, "Communities Slow to Give Women the Credit", *The Western Producer* (August 9, 1984).

In another article, the First National Farm Women's Conference was mentioned: "Research for the conference indicated farm women did not receive the recognition they deserved as farm partners and that many agricultural policies needed to be changed to remove discrimination toward women." Liz Delahey, "A Better Deal for Farm Families is their Goal," *The Western Producer* (July 12, 1984).

113. R.S.C. 1970, c. P18, as amended.

114. Sheila Bean, "Triple Role Taken — Farmer, Co-operator, Agitator," *The Western Producer* (March 21, 1985), p. A42: "Married couples were treated as an individual, while other related partners, such as brother-sister or father-son, were treated as two individuals . . . Brown's letters weren't wasted. Last May, the *Prairie Grain Advance Payments Act* was changed so a husband and wife are each eligible for the sum advanced to individuals. A husband and wife partnership is no longer considered a single unit."

115. *An Act to promote the Development of Agricultural Operations*, S.Q. 1986, c. 54.

116. Mary Jane Lipkin, co-ordinator, Status of Rural Women Project, "Credit Where Credit is Due: Women and Farm Credit in Canada," *First National Farm Women's Conference Background Papers*, Ottawa, December 2-4, 1980, p. 4.

117. For example, the *Act to promote agricultural operations*, one of the statutes administered by the Office

du crédit agricole. Section 14 of the grant application form it uses asks the number of boys over 16 years old on the farm:

(14)The borrower is married / single / a widower or widow / separated / divorced / and has . . . . . dependants of whom . . . . . are children under 16 and . . . . . are boys over 16 living at home.

The borrower is married to . . . . . and they are common as to property / separate as to property / joint owners of acquests.

118. Catherine Meanwell and Susan Glover, *To Have and to Hold — A Guide to Property and Credit Law for Farm Families in Ontario* (Chesley: Concerned Farm Women, 1985).

119. *Parler, c'est se donner du pouvoir. Le pouvoir de se distinguer*, Minutes and report of the general meeting of the Comité des femmes en agriculture de Lanaudière, October 14, 1985, p. 8.

120. *Bank of Montreal* v. *Hancock*, 39 O.R. (2d) 82 (High Court of Ontario).

121. Meanwell and Glover, *To Have and to Hold*, p. 40.

122. For example, see: *Houle* v. *Banque Canadienne Nationale*, S.C. Montreal, May 16, 1983, and the commentary by Paul Martel at (1983) R. du B. 916.

123. Meanwell and Glover, *To Have and to Hold*, pp. 40-41.

124. Quebec, ministère de l'Agriculture, des Pêcheries et de l'Alimentation, *From Sharing the Work to Sharing the Power: Three Year Plan* (Quebec: 1986).

125. On this point generally, see: Rose-Lizée, *Portrait des femmes collaboratrices du Québec*, pp. 120-123.

126. At present, taxpayers may contribute to a registered retirement savings plan for their spouse, but may not exceed the maximum for a single person. Spouses may both take the benefit of the maximum contribution only where there are two separate incomes: Subs. 146(8.2) *Income Tax Act*; s. 924 *Quebec Taxation Act*.

127. See the commentary by Emmanuel Wagner, "La rémunération de la collaboration professionnelle du conjoint," *Recueil Dalloz Sirey*, no. 1 weekly (January 3, 1985), dealing with a similar French statute, *La loi No. 82-695 relative aux conjoints d'artisans et de commercants travaillant dans une entreprise familiale*, July 10, 1982. The report of the working group on "femmes collaboratrices" considered the difficulty inherent in a unilateral declaration. Other more flexible formulae have been suggested, such as the legal regime governing partnerships, Quebec: Ministère du Conseil exécutif, Secrétariat à la condition féminine, Groupe de travail sur la déclaration de statut de la femme collaboratrice, *Femmes collaboratrices: un statut à choisir* (Québec: 1986), pp. 30-33.

128. Quebec: Ministère du Conseil exécutif, *Femmes collaboratrices*, pp. 33-34.

129. *Ibid.*, p. 31.

130. Dion, *Les femmes dans l'agriculture au Québec*, p. 50.

131. On this point generally, see: Jessie Bernard, *The Female World* (New

York: MacMillan Publishing Co,
Inc., 1981). See also: Carol
Gilligan, *In a Different Voice:
Psychological Theory and
Women's Development*
(Cambridge, Mass.: Harvard
University Press, 1982).

132. In a televised interview, Germaine
Greer stated: "The problem is not
that doctors are men, but that
medicine is male." *Realities*, April
24, 1985, TV Ontario.

133. Dion, *Les femmes dans
l'agriculture au Québec*, p. 63.

134. Gloria Steinem, "The Time Factor"
in *Outrageous Acts and Everyday
Rebellions* (New York: Holt,
Rinehart and Winston, 1983), pp.
173-175.

135. Suzanne Dion added a personal
observation: "I noticed that some
women who have attained the
position in agriculture that they
wanted got there after taking some
time off. One had gone on a trip;
another had tried working away
from the farm; another had to take
time off because of illness . . . .
They had had time to think, and
the people around them had
realized that the work they were
doing was important. Everyone
had recognized their importance."
(translation)

Women
as Non-Family
Farmworkers

by Julie Lee

3 TABLE OF CONTENTS

First and foremost, I would like to thank Somer Brodbribb, who acted as my French language consultant and offered tremendous support throughout the writing and research process. I would also like to thank Pamela Smith who shared her expertise and superior understanding of the census data with me. Special thanks go to Marie Patry, of Statistics Canada, for dealing with my anxious telephone calls with utmost patience and helpfulness. And, of course, I wish to acknowledge the assistance and support received from Diane Morissette and Marylee Stephenson, of the Canadian Advisory Council on the Status of Women. Further, Fran Shaver, Mariette Trottier, and Lise Pilon-Lê contributed valuable information toward this research.

Julie Lee

INTRODUCTION

This publication documents the nature and degree of women's support of, and participation in, the Canadian agricultural industry. Most recent studies of women and agriculture have emphasized the invisibility of women partners in the farming enterprise, and the extent to which they have suffered the consequences of invisibility in terms of lost income and status, and increased health risks, family violence, and isolation.

This article, however, deals with another group of women in Canadian agriculture, which, in many ways, is even more invisible than are family farm women. These are women who come to the farm on a daily or seasonal basis to plant, tend, and harvest crops for wages. For purposes of this discussion, these women will be called *non-family* farmworkers. Unfortunately, researchers and policy-makers have paid little attention to this segment of the agricultural work force. Consequently, their circumstances remain obscure — a dangerous situation, given the harsh and inequitable living and working conditions endured by these women.

This article attempts to describe these women and their working and living conditions. The first section considers the economic factors contributing to the phenomenon of non-family farmworkers. It makes a connection between mounting pressures on Canadian family farms and increased demand for non-family farmworkers in certain crops and regions. Official data are also examined in order to demonstrate its limitations in documenting the trends and characteristics of the non-family farmworker labour force. Because of the flawed nature of official data, the last half of this article turns to first-hand accounts of the experiences of these women. Interviews were conducted with farmworkers and farm labour organizations. The farmworkers were non-randomly selected, according to their ability to best represent the broad range of experiences of the female farmworker. Additional insights and information were contributed by the Tolpuddle Farm Labour Information Centre (TFLIC) based in Toronto, Ontario and the Canadian Farmworkers Union (CFU) based in Surrey, British Columbia.

THE CHANGING FACE OF THE FARM AND THE FARMWORKER

The nature of Canadian farming, and the farm community itself, have undergone tremendous, if not revolutionary, changes in the last half of this century. A marked exodus of persons from rural farming communities to urban centres has occurred since the 1930s. There has been a 38% drop in the number of persons employed in agriculture since 1951.[1] Mechanization and industrialization have affected not only the kind of work performed on the farm, but also the scheduling, growing, and marketing of agricultural products. More recently, the small family farm has rapidly lost ground as the most common unit of agricultural production. In Ontario, the number of small- to medium-size farms (3 to 239 acres) decreased by 37% between 1951 and 1976, while the number of larger farms (240 to 1,600 + acres) increased by 24%.[2] Nationally, a decline in the number of smaller farms (under 1,600 acres) occurred at the same time that the number of large farms (over 1,600 acres) increased.[3] In addition, an increasing number of small farm owners contracted or leased their lands and resources to larger farm corporations or food producers. As a result, the number of small farms may have remained constant in the census data, even though their coordination may no longer have been controlled by farm family members. Although small family farms continue to represent the majority of units of agricultural production, Canadian farm families must cope with increasing financial and social pressures in order to survive. The result has been a significant rise in work and stress levels of family farm women.

Prior to the World War II era, farming in Canada was subsistent in nature, the farms typically smaller, and the goods produced principally for the consumption of the farm family, with any surplus being marketed in the local community. James S. Holt, an American agricultural economist, outlines the characteristics of the older, more traditional farm economy:

> For the most part, farming units were diversified enterprises of the size that could be worked by one family. Virtually all the farm's productive resources except land were supplied by the family. The farm family produced for its own

needs and attempted in addition to produce a small saleable surplus to obtain those necessities and an occasional luxury that they could not produce themselves. Where hired labour was used, it generally had to be resident on the farm, and the few larger enterprises that existed were essentially replications of family units.[4]

During the 1960s, however, technological developments in agricultural production, marketing, and transportation broadened the variety of agricultural products that could enter commercial channels.[5] There was a move to production on a larger scale, with profit incentives directing farmers away from traditional mixed farming toward crop specialization. Mixed farming was no longer a profitable venture in the face of the expanding canning and food processing industry. Consequently, in certain regions and crops, there has been a move toward larger farms, increasing crop centralization and specialization, and a resulting demand for staggering increases in capital investment for machinery, chemicals, land, and labour. These changes have been especially pronounced in the fruit and vegetable growing sector, where farming has been moving toward *agribusiness* or *corporate farming*. Erma Stultz, a founding member of the Tolpuddle Farm Labour Information Centre, points out that "cash crop farmers as we have known them are becoming extinct. They are no longer farmers but businessmen, heads of corporations. The nature of agriculture is moving quickly away from farming to factory-type work."[6]

Small family farm operations simply cannot compete in this new economy, and, increasingly, are losing control over their own enterprises. Larger and more powerful agricultural corporations are pressuring small farms to operate in ways that serve their interests rather than those of the farm owners. Farmers are told what to produce, which seeds/seedlings are to be purchased, which chemicals are to be purchased and when and where used, and when the crop is to be harvested. Richard Taves, an Ontario farmer, talks of rising pressure on small farms and increasing loss of control experienced by farmers:

> The family farm is surrounded on all sides by interests that are extremely large. On the one side you sell to interests that are very concentrated and are able to dictate the prices that they're going to pay. The processing industry can pretty well set the terms and conditions whereby farmers are going to sell tomatoes . . . On the other hand, the farmer's inputs are controlled in many cases by the same interests. In tomatoes, for example, the company that

buys the tomatoes also supplies the seedlings, determines the spraying program, often hires the sprayer, decides how many times it's going to be sprayed, and so on. So the farmer has very, very little independence. The rules for both selling and for buying for the farmer are set by the same interests. The opportunity for farm families to get into the tomato industry and make something of it, with one intensive crop like that, is rapidly disappearing. The tendency is, of course, to the larger operator with the expensive equipment.[7]

All of these changes have had an impact on the nature and distribution of agricultural labour. In his 1981 study of the agricultural work force in Quebec, Michel Morisset determines two dominant trends.[8] He argues that the first of these trends occurred between 1931 and 1965. In 1931, family heads of farms made up 51% of the agricultural work force, non-paid family aid accounted for 39%, and salaried farm labour constituted the remaining 10%. However, as a result of the move of rural residents into urban areas, the 1965 statistics look very different. In 1965, family heads of farms had decreased in numbers but had increased their proportion of the agricultural work force to 72%, while family help plummeted to only 13%, from the 1931 total of 39%. Salaried labour, however, also slightly decreased in numbers, to 15% of the agricultural work force. Due to burgeoning industry and technological development, a second trend is seen in the distribution of labour from 1965 to 1979. While numbers of agricultural workers across categories continued to decrease, a marked increase in the numbers of paid labourers had occurred by 1979. Specifically, family heads had dropped to 42% of the agricultural work force by that year. Family non-paid help had risen to 26%. The most significant change was the increase in paid labour to 32% of the work force. Morisset concludes that a concentration of production on farms based more and more on waged agricultural labour, and less and less on the labour of the farm families, occurred.[9] Further research in the area leads Morisset to speculate that the gender-neutral data of Quebec does not reflect the preponderance of women in the salaried farmworker category. He writes:

> For seven or eight years, a new category of farm labour has increased in importance: the salaried worker, who now constitutes about 30% of agricultural labour, traditionally done by the family on the farm. Quebec data is not available to indicate the gender breakdown of employment categories. However, it is likely that a good part of the salaried workers are

women, and that proportionally more of them are seasonal workers.[10]

An examination of the national data supports Morisset's speculation. In a study of 1951 to 1981 census data, combined with data from the 1975 to 1983 Labour Force Survey, Pamela Smith examines trends in the nature of the agricultural work force, including a consideration of gender.[11] Consistent with Morisset's examination of Quebec, Smith finds that self-employed heads of farms moved from 65.6% of the 1951 Canadian agricultural work force to 48.1% in 1981. The category of unpaid family help moved from 17.4% to 8.4% in the same time period. Smith's study also indicates a startling rise in the paid labourer category from 16.6% in 1951 to 43.5% in 1981. This indicates that the increase in the paid labourer sector of the Canadian agricultural work force is a significant and widespread national trend.

When the gender of agricultural workers within each work category is taken into account, the data reveal a clearer picture of the current redistribution of the agricultural work force. Smith finds that:

> . . . both the number of self-employed and unpaid family workers have decreased; unpaid workers have declined at a greater rate, however. Paid labour has increased by 60%. Among males, self-employment has decreased by 50% and unpaid work by 89%. Among females self-employment has increased by 214% and unpaid work by 58%. Male paid workers have increased by 28% and female paid workers by **753%** between 1951 and 1981. By 1981, women represented 68% of those involved in unpaid family agricultural employment, 24% of paid and 10% of self-employed workers.[12]
>
> *(emphasis added)*

Therefore, it is evident that the official statistics clearly indicate an increase in women's involvement in agriculture.

The changing face of the farm economy is most certainly associated with changes in the distribution of the agricultural work force. The most significant of these changes has been the sharp increase in the female paid work category. However, unlike the Agriculture Population Linkage used by Pamela Smith, the Population Census does not tell us whether these women are family or non-family farmworkers. Given the increasing financial pressures on the farm family, it is likely that more farm partners/spouses are reporting salaries in order to establish personal economic security, or for tax purposes. What, then, is the face of the female non-family farmworker? What differentiates her from the family paid worker?

Both the TFLIC and the CFU described the typical non-family farmworker as being (1) a woman, (2) from a racial minority, and (3) a poor person. The TFLIC reports estimates of 70,000 to 150,000 full-time and seasonal farmworkers in Ontario. Of these, they have estimated that 60% are women.[13] In British Columbia, the only other province with an organization dealing specifically with farmworker issues, Raj Chouhan, president of the CFU, reports 18,000 to 20,000 full-time and seasonal farmworkers, with women comprising 70% of this group.[14] These organizations base their estimates of the numbers of non-family farmworkers on examination of official data supplemented with the benefits of repeated and direct field research. Other than gender, then, there are three variables that differentiate non-family farmworkers from family farmworkers. These are: crop or region; ethnicity; and economic status.

Crop or region must be considered because there is a high concentration of female non-family farmworker participation associated with the production of certain crops in particular regions. Generally, cash crop agriculture, such as fruits, vegetables, mushrooms, and tobacco, are associated with an increased demand for hired farmworkers. In contrast to the popular perception of a small team of male farmhands on a dairy or wheat farm, this kind of agricultural production requires large crews of 20 to 100 farmworkers (who happen to be mostly women) working in the

fields or mushroom factories. Typically, these crops require more
intensive manual labour, since they have resisted mechanized harvesting.
These are also the crops whose production has become the most
centralized and specialized. Usually these crop production areas are in
regions close to urban centres. This is important because the growers
depend upon this proximity in order to draw on a relatively consistent
source of farm labour.

> In general, there tend to be more hired workers than family workers in areas
> of extensive irrigation where fruits and vegetables are the leading crops, in
> the vicinity of large metropolitan areas where horticultural operations are
> concentrated, and in those plantation and ranching areas where units have
> always been larger than could be handled by a single family.[15]

Ethnicity is also an important variable associated with female non-
family farmworkers. In the United States, researchers have noted the
longstanding tradition of hiring ethnic minorities for farmwork.

> Wage-earning women have continuously contributed to agricultural produc-
> tion in the West. Women hired as laborers have been newly arrived European
> immigrants, blacks, Asians, Chicanos, . . . Black women, immigrant women,
> and poor women have performed extensive agricultural labour. These women
> have worked in the fields when fieldwork for middle or upper class white
> women was considered inappropriate.[16]

In Canada, similar ethnic hiring patterns exist. The results of research
and advocacy work by CFU and TFLIC indicate that the majority of non-
family farmworkers are new immigrants from Portugal, India, Asia,
Latin America, and Mexico. In 1984, the Tolpuddle Centre conducted a
study of farmworkers in southwestern Ontario, which found that there
were increasing numbers of Latin American farmworkers.[17] Many of
these workers were Salvadoreans who had recently come to Canada.

The majority of non-family farmworkers are women belonging to
racial minorities who, as a group, have low incomes. This is not a
surprising situation, since we know that both sexism and racism
contribute to employment and wage discrimination. Ironically, it is a
cyclical kind of situation, where farmwork reinforces the poverty that is
already a problem for ethnic women. Many immigrant women, lacking
proficiency in either of Canada's official languages, or unable to meet
Canadian educational criteria, turn to farmwork for employment, where
they are paid extremely poor wages. In fact, farmwork is the lowest-paid
occupation in the entire occupational spectrum. A high proportion of this

work is remunerated on a piece-work basis, wherein workers are paid by the number of bushels/sacks picked. There is provincial variation in terms of guaranteeing farmworkers minimum wages; however, "farm labour has traditionally been excluded from the application of the minimum wage legislation."[18] Despite the fact that the federal minimum wage for employees over 17 years of age is $3.50 an hour,[19] vegetable-, fruit-, and mushroom-pickers receive an average of only $2.00 to $3.00 per hour.

An examination of the official census data finds that there is almost no representation of paid farmworkers with the characteristics outlined above. Statistics Canada breaks down the paid farmworker category into four distinct sub-categories. These are: crop farm workers, nursery and related workers, farm machinery operators, and others involved in farming work and animal husbandry. These categories are also broken down in terms of gender; breakdowns by province and ethnicity are also available.

One of the primary circumstances of female non-family farmworkers is that they are more likely to be working in cash crops as harvesters, cultivators, or planters than are male non-family farmworkers. Table 1 indicates that the crop farm worker category closely corresponds with the definition of the work most typically performed by non-family farmworkers. This category consists of people employed in cash crop agriculture, performing tasks such as cultivating, transplanting, and harvesting. Generally, these people are identified as berry-pickers, tobacco-primers, greenhouse workers, or fruit-pickers. Based on the exploratory data collected by the farmworker organizations, one would expect 60% to 70% of these workers to be women. In fact, the majority, though a smaller proportion than anticipated, of these agricultural workers are women (53%). In comparison, women are significantly underrepresented in the other categories of farmwork, i.e., nursery and gardening workers (17.5%) and farm machinery operators (14%). Only in horticulture and animal husbandry are more balanced ratios of women to men found, with women representing 42.5% of this category. These women are more likely to be family farmworkers, since this category is associated with family-maintained livestock and mixed farming enterprises. Overall, then, we find that the national data indicate that women are more likely to be cash crop farmworkers, but do not reflect the high proportion that data from the farmworker organizations led us to expect

(60% to 70%) within this category of paid farmwork. If this group of female crop workers included a representative sample of non-family workers, significantly higher numbers of them would be expected. Moreover, at this point in examination of the official data, it is still uncertain whether the figures represent family or non-family paid farmworkers.

It is necessary, then, to consider whether the official data reflect the regional characteristics associated with female non-family farmwork. According to reports from the CFU and the TFLIC, most intensive, paid non-family labour areas are in Ontario and British Columbia, and, to a lesser extent, in Quebec and Manitoba. Within each of these provinces are regions characterized by a high concentration of specialized cash crops. For example, the Fraser Valley in British Columbia is known for highly concentrated fruit and vegetable production. Similarly, agricultural production in southwestern Ontario focusses primarily on fruit, vegetable, and tobacco. Taking Ontario and British Columbia as examples, then, high concentrations of crop farm workers would be expected in these provinces.

In fact, it is found that British Columbia and Ontario, combined, claim 60% of all Canadian crop farm workers. (See Table 2.) Also, 57.5% of British Columbian and Ontarian workers are women. (See Table 3.) In each of these provinces, this category includes the highest representation of female farmworkers. Nevertheless, these numbers do not reflect the numbers of non-family farmworkers reported by the farm labour organizations. In Ontario, the Tolpuddle Centre estimates a total of 150,000 non-family farmworkers approximately 90,000 (60%) of whom are women. In contrast, the data across all farmworker categories in Ontario show only a total of 84,595 paid farmworkers, 29,310 (35%) of whom are women. Again, the official data do not reflect the characteristics associated with the population of female non-family farmworkers.

Finally, an examination of ethnic variation across categories of paid farmwork indicates that female non-family farmworkers are not well represented in the official data. As indicated earlier, female non-family farmworkers are usually drawn from ethnic minorities. The ethnic groups most frequently associated with this work are Portuguese, East Indian, Asian, and South and Central American. However, an examination of Table 4 shows that these characteristic ethnic groups are significantly underrepresented in comparison to Other European groups (France,

Table 1: Gender breakdown of farm owners/workers (Family and non-family)

Gender	Livestock Owners/Operators[a]		Crop Owners/Operators[b]		Crop Farm Workers[c]		Nursery & Gardening Workers[d]		Farm Machinery Operators[e]		Other Farm Workers, Horticul. & Animal Husbandry[f]	
	No.	%	No.	%	No.	%	No.	%	No.	%	No.	%
Female	5,255	12.1	4,190	9.5	28,680	52.7	13,385	17.5	1,853	14.0	35,335	41.5
Male	38,035	87.9	39,915	90.5	25,715	47.3	63,060	82.5	11,425	86.0	49,835	58.5
Total	43,290	100	44,105	100	54,395	100	76,445	100	13,278	100	85,170	100

Source: Canada, Statistics Canada, 1981 Census, Special Tabulation, 1985.

Notes:

(a) Livestock Owners/Operators: Occupation concerned with owning, operating a livestock farm.

Activities include: caring for, training, shipping, etc. livestock, growing food crops for livestock, etc. (e.g., dairy farm, pig farm, beef cattle farm, etc.).

(b) Crop Owners/Operators: Occupation concerned with owning, operating cash crop farm.

Activities include: producing vegetables, grains, fruit, mushrooms, generally horticultural plants.

(c) Crop Farm Workers: Occupation primarily concerned with growing and harvesting cash crops (vegetables, mushrooms, tobacco, fruit, etc.).

Activities include: cultivating, transplanting, seeding, cultivating, pruning, harvesting, (e.g., berry-picker, tobacco primer, greenhouse worker, fruit-picker, etc.).

(d) Nursery & Related Workers: Unique group with the occupation concerned with planting and growing trees, shrubs and ornamental plants, providing landscaping, gardening, and groundskeeping.

Activities include: preparing soil, transplanting sod, shrubs, plants, etc., pruning, etc.

(e) Farm Machinery Operators: Occupation concerned with operating farm machinery.

Activities include: operating tractors, self-propelled equipment, cultivators, combines, crop spraying machines, etc.

(f) Other Farming Work: Occupations in farmwork not elsewhere classified concerned with general farming, horticultural, and animal husbandry.

Activities include: packing eggs, spraying and tending Christmas trees, irrigation, caring for research animals, etc.

Table 2: Provincial distribution of farmworkers (Family and non-family)

Provinces	Crop Farm Workers		Nursery & Related Workers		Farm Machinery Operators		Other Farm Workers, Hort. & An. Husb.		Total Male		Total Female		Total	
	No.	% (of natl.)	No.	%	No.	%	No.	%	No.	%	No.	%	No.	%
Prince Edward Island	1,185	2.2	450	0.6	315	2.4	830	1.0	1,985	1.3	795	1.0	2,780	1.2
Newfoundland	180	0.3	870	1.1	60	0.5	285	0.3	1,140	0.8	255	0.3	1,395	0.6
Nova Scotia	1,080	2.0	2,665	3.5	285	2.1	1,685	2.0	4,170	2.8	1,545	2.0	5,715	2.5
New Brunswick	1,690	3.1	1,820	2.4	395	3.0	1,005	1.2	3,535	2.4	1,375	1.7	4,910	2.1
Quebec	5,890	10.8	14,020	18.3	845	6.4	9,535	11.2	24,130	16.1	6,160	7.8	30,290	13.2
Ontario	27,005	49.6	31,380	41.0	5,025	37.9	21,185	24.9	55,285	36.9	29,310	37.0	84,595	36.9
Manitoba	2,975	5.5	3,300	4.3	1,385	10.4	9,095	10.7	11,140	7.4	5,615	7.1	16,755	7.3
Saskatchewan	5,300	9.7	2,875	3.8	1,975	14.9	16,995	20.0	15,025	10.0	12,120	15.3	27,145	11.8
Alberta	3,805	7.0	8,175	10.7	2,025	15.3	19,665	23.1	19,680	13.1	13,990	17.7	33,670	14.7
British Columbia	5,275	10.0	10,790	14.1	950	7.2	4,865	5.7	13,855	9.2	8,025	10.1	21,880	9.5
Yukon	5	0	50	.1	0	0	10	0	40	0	25	0	65	0
Northwest Territories	5	0	50	.1	0	0	15	0	50	0	20	0	70	0
Canada	54,395	100	76,445	100	13,260	100	85,170	100	150,035	100	79,235	100	229,270	100

Source: Canada, Statistics Canada, Long Form Census Operations, 1981 Census, Special Statistical Tabulation, 1985.

Table 3: Provincial distribution of farmworkers, by gender

Provinces	Crop Farm Workers		Nursery & Related Workers		Farm Machinery Operators		Other Farm Workers, Horticl., Anim. Husb.	
	No.	%	No.	%	No.	%	No.	%
Prince Edward Island								
Female	525	44	45	10	55	17	170	20
Male	660	56	405	90	260	83	660	80
Total Sex	1,185	100	450	100	315	100	830	100
Newfoundland								
Female	50	28	140	16	5	8	60	21
Male	130	72	730	84	55	92	225	79
Total Sex	180	100	870	100	60	100	285	100
Nova Scotia								
Female	485	45	495	19	0	0	565	34
Male	595	55	2,170	81	285	100	1,120	66
Total Sex	1,080	100	2,665	100	285	100	1,685	100
New Brunswick								
Female	760	45	280	15	35	9	300	30
Male	930	55	1,540	85	360	91	705	70
Total Sex	1,690	100	1,820	100	395	100	1,005	100
Quebec								
Female	2,470	42	1,130	8	90	11	2,470	26
Male	3,420	58	12,890	92	755	89	7,065	74
Total Sex	5,890	100	14,020	100	845	100	9,535	100
Ontario								
Female	15,435	57	5,095	16	780	16	8,000	38
Male	11,570	43	26,285	84	4,245	84	13,185	62
Total Sex	27,005	100	31,380	100	5,025	100	21,185	100
Manitoba								
Female	1,335	45	440	13	125	9	3,715	41
Male	1,640	55	2,860	87	1,260	91	5,380	59
Total Sex	2,975	100	3,300	100	1,385	100	9,095	100
Saskatchewan								
Female	2,565	48	610	21	330	17	8,615	51
Male	2,735	52	2,265	79	1,645	83	8,380	49
Total Sex	5,300	100	2,875	100	1,975	100	16,995	100
Alberta								
Female	1,985	52	2,445	30	305	15	9,255	47
Male	1,820	48	5,730	70	1,720	85	10,410	53
Total Sex	3,805	100	8,175	100	2,025	100	19,665	100
British Columbia								
Female	3,060	58	2,680	25	110	12	2,175	45
Male	2,215	42	8,110	75	840	88	2,690	55
Total Sex	5,275	100	10,790	100	950	100	4,865	100
Yukon								
Female	5	100	15	30	0	0	5	50
Male	0	0	35	70	0	0	5	50
Total Sex	5	100	50	100	0	0	10	100
Northwest Territories								
Female	5	100	10	20	0	0	5	33
Male	0	0	40	80	0	0	10	67
Total Sex	5	100	50	100	0	0	15	100
Canada								
Female	28,680	53	13,385	18	1,835	14	35,335	41
Male	25,715	47	63,060	82	11,425	86	49,835	59
Total Sex	54,395	100	76,445	100	13,260	100	85,170	100

Source: Canada, Statistics Canada, Long Form Census Operations, Special Tabulation, 1985.

Table 4: Farm labourers aged 15 years of age and over by selected occupations, sex, and selected ethnic origin, for Canada, the provinces, and territories, 1981 census

	Crop Farm Workers	Nursery & Related Workers	Farm Machinery Operators	Other Farm Workers, Hort., An. Hus. Occs. Nec.
TOTAL SEX				
Total – Ethnic Origin	54,360	76,430	13,230	85,165
Mexican	50	20	5	10
Other South American	50	110	15	30
Portuguese-Italian & Greek	2,180	4,735	145	1,105
Other European	36,275	47,110	9,935	62,080
West Asian & North African	1,420	430	70	640
Far East Asian & Other	945	940	10	505
Others*	13,440	23,085	3,050	20,795
MALE				
Total – Ethnic Origin	25,710	63,050	11,405	49,835
Mexican	30	15	5	5
Other South American	35	85	15	10
Portuguese-Italian & Greek	815	4,275	145	425
Other European	16,725	37,980	8,585	34,830
West Asian & North African	355	245	65	245
Far East Asian & Other	390	780	10	255
Others*	7,360	19,670	2,580	14,065
FEMALE				
Total – Ethnic Origin	28,650	13,380	1,825	35,330
Mexican	20	5	—	5
Other South American	15	25	—	20
Portuguese-Italian & Greek	1,365	460	—	680
Other European	19,550	9,130	1,350	27,250
West Asian & North African	1,065	185	5	395
Far East Asian & Other	555	160	—	250
Others*	6,080	3,415	470	6,730

Source: Statistics Canada, 1981 Census Data, Special Tabulation, 1985.

Note: * Others = Canadian and United States origins.

England, Germany, etc.) and Others (Canadian and United States origins). If the crop farm worker totals for Mexican, Other South American, Portuguese-Italian and Greek, West Asian and North African, and Far East Asian and Others are combined, it is seen that women represent 65% of these ethnic sub-groups. However, the total representation of this group accounts for only 8.5% of crop farm workers.

With respect to the official data, then, female non-family farmworkers are not represented in terms of their true characteristics and numbers. It seems more likely that family farmworkers, rather than non-family farmworkers, are reported in the census data. Moreover, it is not surprising that non-family farmworkers are underreported in all Canadian regions, since the nature of farmwork itself contributes to the obscurity of this group of workers. Specifically, the seasonality of farmwork results in underreporting, since seasonal farmworkers often work in non-agricultural jobs in the off-season, and are more likely to report this work than the farmwork. Also, as is the case with many family farm women, female farmworkers are more likely to see their work as secondary or unimportant, and tend not to look at their seasonal jobs as "real" work. Further, a number of non-family farmworkers are often transients, moving from province to province, following certain crops. As a result, these individuals are not likely to be picked up in the census data. Given the problems with the official data, first-hand accounts of female farmworkers, as seen in the following sections of this article, give a more accurate view of their living and working experiences.

Legislative Exclusions

Farmworkers are often excluded from crucial and basic protective legislation, which is afforded every other worker in this country. Specifically, farmworkers have been excluded, either totally or partially, from important employment legislation designed to protect the worker's rights to regulation of hours of work, minimum wages, overtime, and access to vacation pay. They are also subject to discriminatory provisions of the *Unemployment Insurance Act* and occupational health and safety policies across the country. In Alberta and Ontario, farmworkers are excluded from labour legislation, which guarantees the rights to organize or form a union in order to improve working conditions. For example, Section 2 of the *Ontario Labour Relations Act* excludes agricultural workers from the definition of employees, thus denying them the protection of that Act in collective bargaining. This results in denial of their rights of freedom of association under the *Charter of Rights and Freedoms*. Mutale Chanda, a former Canadian Farmworker's Union (Ontario) organizer, attributes the reticence of government (provincial and federal) to guarantee farmworkers legislative protection to an outdated perception of agriculture, which holds that farming is a family affair.[20] Generally, it is perceived that farm labour is comprised primarily of family members, and that it therefore makes little sense to legislate labour protection. In relation to legislative protection, a spokesperson for the Canadian Labour Congress writes:

> What most concerns the Canadian Labour Congress is the undeniable fact that most provincial labour legislation today enshrines the concept of the seasonal farm worker as an inferior human being. This should not be taken as an accusation that they are everywhere treated as inferior by their employers; only that they are legally designated as such by lawmakers who (have) had neither the courage nor the imagination to tackle the problems associated with the peculiar nature of agricultural employment.[21]

For example, before 1983, Section 16 of the *Unemployment Insurance Compensation Act* required farmworkers to work 25 days with one employer in order to qualify for UIC benefits. This was seen by farmworker organizations as a highly discriminatory piece of legislation, inasmuch as no other Canadian worker had the same qualification criteria. Further, the 25-day requirement directly benefitted large growers and their demands for labour, at the same time that this provision restricted the rights of the farmworker. If the farmworker objected to the working conditions on a particular farm s/he was not free to leave since s/he would lose qualification credits. Also, this requirement benefitted larger growers' agreements with labour contractors, who supply them with groups of workers on a regular basis.[22] In response to the farmworkers' protests, the Minister of Immigration and Employment promised to revise this section so that farmworkers would be treated equally under the Act. In fact, as of July 1, 1983, the 25-day requirement for farmworkers was dropped. However, within two months, the major growers and producers across Canada lobbied to have the requirement reinstated. Finally, in March 1984, the government bowed to the powerful lobby of agribusiness representatives, and a new seven-day requirement was put in place. Although less than the 25-day constraint, the seven-day UIC requirement still exemplifies discriminatory legislative policy, which has a distinctly negative impact on the farmworker.

Farmworkers are also exempt from protection under health and safety legislation in Ontario, British Columbia, and Alberta. This is an especially problematic exclusion, since farming is the third-most-dangerous occupation after mining and logging.[23] In the case of health and safety legislation, farm owners/operators and non-family farmworkers strongly disagree about appropriate legislative response.[24] Part of this resistance may well arise from farmers' traditional opposition to most forms of government intervention. This is ironic, since farmers are becoming more and more controlled by marketing boards and larger processing and pesticide industries.

British Columbia's revisions to the *Workers Compensation Board Act* demonstrate the same pattern of discriminatory application of legislation. In 1984, this Act was revised to include farmworkers. This was seen as a step in the right direction, since the consequences of losing paid time due to workplace injury or illness can be profound for the already-poor population of non-family farmworkers. However, the revisions to the *Workers Compensation Board Act* exclude farmworkers from health and safety regulations specified by the Act. More

specifically, British Columbia regulation 275/84 under the Act states that the health and safety regulations will be used *only as guidelines* for educational programs relating to health and safety in the farming industry until appropriate regulations are developed. Because no direct regulations under the Act are provided for health and safety protection of farmworkers, they cannot civilly sue their employers for wages lost as a result of health and safety reasons.

Finally, farmworkers in general are faced with discriminatory labour standards legislation. Cash crop farmworkers are set apart from other categories of farmworkers under particularly harsh and sexist employment standards discrimination. For example, Quebec excludes many types of farmworkers from minimum wage provisions, but not nursery workers and tree-planters.[25] Saskatchewan exempts egg hatcheries, greenhouses, and nurseries from the definition of farming, ranching, or market gardening.[26] British Columbia[27] and Ontario[28] set a special, substandard wage for fruit-, vegetable-, and tobacco-pickers, but not for other agricultural workers (including nursery workers). This discrimination directly affects the status of women farmworkers, since women predominate in the cash crop farmworker category. As Table 3 indicates, the categories of farmwork **most** affected by employment standards discrimination are the ones that contain significant majorities of women.

Sexism

In addition to sexism inherent in the legislative discrimination already discussed, female non-family farmworkers also face sexist hiring practices. Women are pressured into cash crop labour and discouraged from working in other, higher-paying categories of farmwork. This labour pattern is based on sexist perceptions of a woman's relation to the family and to work, which maintains that her chief role in society is as a mother and wife, subordinate to her husband, and to men in general. This traditional view of women extends to their role in the work force (if any). Thus, if women do go out into the work force, many of them will continue to play out their subordinate family role, accepting without question that their work is only secondary, and therefore deserving of unfair wages and poor working conditions.

In the case of cash crop farmwork, corporate farms and private farmers openly state that they have policies for hiring more women in lower-paying harvest work.[29] They base this policy on their experiences that women complain less, work longer hours, and are less likely to want to join labour or union organizations. Unfortunately, for these women, their often subordinate role in the family can reinforce their acceptance of poor working conditions. In fact, their employers rely upon the pervasiveness of sexist attitudes in order to access "a dependable, low-cost, docile, readily available, invisible, and temporary labour source."[30]

At the same time, women are less likely to be hired in higher-paying sectors of agricultural work such as nursery work, operating farm machinery, or tree-planting. At least two factors contribute to women's underrepresentation in these jobs. The first has to do with the same sexist attitudes noted above. Micheline and Jeanne, two Québecois seasonal agricultural workers with six to seven years' experience in tree-planting and fruit-picking, attest to the sexist hiring practices of tree-planting contractors. Both of these women were refused employment by many Quebec contractors who have made it a policy not to hire women.[31] As a result, they travel annually to the forests of British Columbia, where women are more frequently hired for this work. Nevertheless, in British Columbia, they still encounter sexist attitudes. For them, continuing this work has meant a constant struggle to prove themselves again and again. In Jeanne's words, "I had to really fight just to get hired," and "when you do prove yourself by producing as much, or more, then the guys, they just don't believe you."[32] On one occasion, Jeanne and another woman were hired as tree-planters in Quebec. However, they were told:

> If you two girls don't plant 600 trees today, you're going to be out. It was only the two girls that he said that to. It's because they don't believe that girls can do that work. There's this whole big rhetoric about the fathers being the heads of families, and guys need these jobs to support their families. They don't think that girls need the money.[33]

The other factor that restricts women's access to higher-paying farmwork is the relationship between their traditional child-care responsibilities and the regional nature of this work. For example, tree-planting usually requires that the workers camp out in the forest for extended periods of time in areas that are far removed from cities and towns. Consequently, it is rare to find mothers doing this kind of work.[34] The contractor makes no provisions for child care and the dangerous and distant nature of this work dissuade mothers from taking their children with them. It is no surprise, then, that Micheline and Jeanne report that a typical tree-planting crew is made up of 25 to 30 men and only 3 to 7 women.[35]

Mothering responsibilities also present serious problems for cash crop farmworkers. Although they work in agricultural areas closer to home, they cannot afford child care, or find that there are no local child-care facilities available to them. As a result, many of these women are forced to take their children — as young as four or five — into the fields with them. If the children are old enough, they work with their mothers in the fields. Otherwise, the mothers must constantly keep an eye on their children while working. This is a serious concern for both family and non-family farm women, since a larger number of children than adults are injured or killed on farm sites. For example, a 1981-1984 Ontario study of farm fatalities indicated that 14% of all farm-associated deaths were of children.[36]

Sexism also gives rise to sexual violence in the farmwork setting. The Canadian Farmworker's Union reports that cases of sexual harassment are skyrocketing, and that it is extremely difficult to protect its members. The many barriers to women's legal protection and recourse, their poverty, and their subordinate position in relation to men further complicate their isolation when they are victims of sexual harassment. In fact, in many cases it would be more accurate to call this violence sexual assault rather than harassment. For example, a Salvadorean vegetable harvester working in southwestern Ontario was repeatedly grabbed by the breasts and genitals by her crew foreman. When she protested to him, he exposed his genitals to her, and had a "good laugh" with other male farmworkers.[37] This woman took her complaint further to the farm owner who told her "not to tolerate that behaviour from the foreman" and that "only he, the owner, had a right to do that kind of stuff." Although it may not be advisable to respond to this kind of violence in kind, Jeanne describes the action that she was forced to take in order to deal with a situation of sexual harassment:

> A couple of times I had to be really violent with a couple of guys. These guys were hassling and coming at me. I ended up having to hit one of them with my shovel. He had a sore back for a week. It was the only thing I could do! That really shocked them, though. It made the guys question themselves.[38]

Health Hazards

It is a fundamental contradiction that farmwork is excluded from health and safety regulations, since farmwork is associated with such a dangerous work environment. Farm families and non-family farmworkers alike are at high risk, given that they work with pesticides and farm equipment on a daily basis. Micheline describes the farmworker's extremely close contact with pesticides and some of the effects:

> While picking cherries in British Columbia I had, for about three weeks, a sort of rash and a real itch on my arms. Now with apple picking I started to have bronchitis, and then later on it turned into asthma. I wasn't able to finish the picking season because I couldn't breathe enough. But everybody has some kind of reaction to apples. You start off by sneezing . . . everybody. Apples or cherries, when you're doing the picking you're always hearing somebody sneezing. Because when you're doing the picking you cause the dust from the pesticides to come up; you stir it up. You're moving the tree, you're moving the branches, and so the dust is stirred up and you breathe it because it's in the air. After the third day working in apples it was like I had smoked two packages of cigarettes. I was really coughing. And, just to clear my lungs before going to sleep, I had to cough a lot . . . It's a real problem because you're out there working with nature and at the same time you're working with an awful lot of chemical products.[39]

Working conditions on the farm serve to further exacerbate already dangerous pesticide situations. For example, only rarely do farm owners provide farmworkers with on-site washing facilities.[40] As a result, farmworkers eat their lunches and suppers with hands still covered with pesticides from the crop they have been working. This kind of neglect is not a reflection of malice on the part of the farmer. On the contrary, farmers may not understand the dangers of pesticides. They themselves are in danger as a result of exposure to high concentrations of agricultural chemicals while spraying. It is typical for farmers not to make use of protective clothing. Clearly, there is a need to train and educate the farmer and farmworkers with respect to proper handling of farm chemicals.

There is also a need for an improved understanding of pesticides and their effects on Canadian society in general. As consumers, the Canadian population is affected by the increasing use of agricultural chemicals. Raj Chouhan provides an example:

We have seen a field of broccoli sprayed and the workers were asked to pick it right away, even though the leaves were still wet with pesticides. The broccoli was loaded on a truck and we (CFU researchers) followed it. It was taken to a roadside vegetable market and sold right away. People just don't know what they're eating. There was no sign to say "please wash it before you eat it."[41]

Despite the fact that two British Columbia farmworkers were proven to have died as a result of pesticide poisonings, no protective or corrective action has been taken. In both cases, the coroner's inquest jury made strong recommendations that immediate changes be made in order to strengthen health and safety regulations.[42] Generally, the rural health-care system is inadequately equipped to deal with farm chemical-related issues.[43] Even in urban centres, medical personnel lack the expertise to properly diagnose and treat victims of pesticide poisonings. Often the symptoms associated with these poisonings mirror allergic, influenza-like infections, or nervous disorders. Blood and urine testing facilities, often the only diagnostic tool appropriate in these cases, are rarely used, and often are inaccessible to rural areas.

The Canadian Environmental Law Association has drafted a brief which includes many important recommendations for pesticide policy revision.[44] As a result of their study of the problem, they have agreed upon an extensive package of recommendations, which state that government should:

. . . authorize public access to all pesticide health and safety data; require public participation in registration, re-evaluation and regulation-making as well as court access; and authorize automatic suspension or cancellation of registered pesticides where the safety tests supporting registration are shown to be invalid.

Reforms to improve government authority to act as well as allow greater public access to the regulatory and judicial processes with respect to pesticides, are outlined in this paper. Considering the potential damage to human health and the environment from improperly registered, used or disposed-of pesticides, it is clear that legislative improvements to both the governmental authority to act and the role of the public in the process are past due.[45]

Racism
Racism has a major impact on the hiring of farmworkers. Clearly, there is

a link between racism and the high numbers of non-family farmworkers who are women of colour. Moreover, many immigrant women are denied access to community participation and the full range of occupational choices because they lack proficiency in either of the official languages. New immigrant women, who enter Canada in the family class or assisted relative class, are restricted in their access to training allowances for some French or English language-training programs. These restrictions are primarily based on the perception that women will have no need of language training, since they will remain in the home. Therefore, men tend to have better access to programs for learning either French or English. Community attitudes and cultural practices also reinforce this situation. As a result, immigrant women remain socially isolated in their homes, and if they must work, they are forced to take racially ghettoized employment, such as cash crop farmwork.

Racism is also an issue for non-immigrant farmworkers. For example, there are often discriminatory practices openly exercised against native Canadian farmworkers. In southwestern Ontario, many native Canadians have been refused employment on purely racist grounds. As a result, an association of native Canadians formed a native farmworker collective in an attempt to fight this discrimination. (A similar program exists in the Manitoba sugar-beet industry.) This collective signed a contract with local grape producers agreeing to provide the producers with a crew of workers, their transportation, clothing, and picking supplies. However, the native farmworkers were subjected to racist attitudes and practices by the farm owners and the association decided to abandon the project.

In some cases, larger growers have been known to segregate the farmwork force on the basis of race:

> The orchard on the other side of the street, it was just Native Canadians who worked there. I don't know why, but over there they just used Native Canadians. I don't know if it's because they can pay them less or what. And then there are places that just use Hindu people. I always end up working with other people from Québec.[46]

The Canadian Farmworker's Union discovered that this practice of segregating workers on the basis of ethnicity was for the purposes of paying one ethnic group less than the average wage.[47] Segregation prevented the lower-paid workers from comparing notes with the other workers.

> Farmwork is hard, back-breaking work. We gotta be out there in the fields in the sun, rain, and cold — from six each morning 'til five, six or seven at night. We plant, weed, and when the season comes we pick the crop. At harvest time we work seven days a week.[48]

> Everybody has to overcome themselves. Everybody has to get up at 5:00 in the morning. Sometimes it's zero temperature, and it's raining. And when you get out to the place you're supposed to work, it's snowing. It's cold, it's six o'clock in the morning and there you are until five o'clock in the afternoon.[49]

In addition to the issues already discussed, non-family farmworkers work very hard under extreme working conditions. Further, the piece-work structure pushes them to work harder and faster, with the consequence that these farmworkers are more susceptible to accidents and body strain:

> Apple picking is paid by the bin. You get $12.00 for each bin that you pick. Usually, people only pick two a day. But if you're really desperate for money, you might push yourself to pick three. At the same time the picking conditions are so impossible that it's difficult to fill a bin. That way it doesn't end up to be very well-paying. The trees are not well pruned and instead of giving you a sack that ties around your body they give you a pail. You have to hang on to the pail with one hand and pick apples with the other hand. It's also more dangerous because, with one hand, you're more likely to fall. It's hard to hold your balance.[50]

Also, the piece-work basis of agricultural work, emphasizing quantity rather than quality, displaces the superior benefits of attention to the environment and ecology. Both Jeanne and Micheline strongly recommend that farmworkers be paid on a salary, rather than piece-work basis. In Jeanne's experience, she

> . . . could see that women were much better in terms of the quality of the work produced. I could see that. I think it's in their bones. I mean, I like money just like the guys do. But it's not a fixed idea with women while they're working. I've already talked to some of the other women about it. We're not thinking about the quantity we're producing.

> I really like the work I'm doing, and I think of it at the ecological level, too. So it would be a lot better for women if the pay was by the hour, instead of by quantity of production.

You're supposed to reach 85% quality in your work in order to get paid. If a guy plants, at 70% quality, 2,000 trees a day at 8¢ a tree, he makes $160.00. But he's only planted 70% quality. Whereas for me, I plant 1,000 trees a day at 100% quality. His quality will average 85%, of course, but he gets paid more than I do. And, of course, the trees he plants die, a lot of them die.[51]

CONCLUSION

In summary, the plight of Canadian non-family farmworker women is dismal. Much needs to be said about the courage and stamina of these women. Although the agricultural economy relies heavily on them for the essential work that they do, their labour is not recognized as the very backbone of cash crop production. Further, they are not protected from severe and dangerous working conditions. The mythology surrounding agriculture has us believe that there couldn't be a healthier place than "down on the farm," when, in fact, agricultural work means exposure to dangerous chemicals and farm equipment. We also believe that we are eating fresh uncontaminated foods. Unfortunately, though, this is often not the case. As a result of the emphasis on quantity over quality, a sharp increase is seen in the use of agricultural chemicals. Canadians can no longer turn a blind eye to the situation of farmworkers, or to trends in the agricultural economy. Women are being used as cheap, exploited, and unprotected farm labour.

Changes have to occur at all levels of society. The removal of discriminatory policies and legislation, which serve to marginalize and silence non-family farmworkers, is the first step. Further, there is an urgent need for more research on these issues. Official data collection procedures are flawed, and consequently obscure or render invisible the participation of women in farmwork. This is a critical gap in knowledge, since so many policy decisions rest upon an examination of official data.

Finally, much could be gained from the recognition of interests shared by non-family and family farm women. The vital contribution of both groups to the agricultural economy is ignored. They are sisters in terms of their concerns about child care, health and safety, sexual violence, and economic security. Clearly, all of these women are struggling on common ground in order to survive in this new agricultural economy.

1. Pamela Smith, " 'Not Enough Hours, Our Accountant Tells Me': Trends in Children's, Women's and Men's Involvement in Canadian Agriculture," presented to the Annual Meeting of the Canadian Agricultural Economics and Farm Management Society, University of Prince Edward Island, Charlottetown, June 26, 1985, p. 8.

2. Linda Harasim and Lucio Teles, *Farmworkers: the Invisible Minority in Ontario: An Introduction for the Public* (Toronto: Tolpuddle Farm Labour Information Centre, 1983).

3. Canada, Statistics Canada, Censuses of Agriculture, 1901-1981.

4. James S. Holt, "Introduction to the Seasonal Farm Labor Problem," in *Seasonal Agricultural Labor Markets in the United States*, ed. Robert D. Emerson (Ames, Iowa: Iowa State University Press, 1984), p. 5.

5. Holt, "Introduction to the Seasonal Farm Labour Problem," p. 6.

6. Erma Stultz, founding member of Tolpuddle Farm Labour Information Centre, 692 Coxwell Avenue, Toronto, Ontario, taped interview, December 1985.

   The Tolpuddle Farm Labour Information Centre, formerly known as the Ontario Farm Labour Information Centre, works to improve the living and working conditions of farmworkers. Most of the centre's work is focussed on ensuring the availability and accessibility of legal and health and safety information. Given the ethnic characteristics of farmworkers, however, the centre is careful to present information pamphlets and publications in the characteristic first languages of farmworkers (i.e., Portuguese, Spanish, French, etc.). This centre is named in recognition of the historic "Tolpuddle Martyrs." Specifically, in 1834, six men were deported from England for their attempts to improve the working conditions of British farmworkers. Eventually, five of these men settled and lived out their lives in southwestern Ontario.

7. Richard Taves, video interview sequence in *To Pick Is Not To Choose*, directed by John Greyson and Toni Venturi, produced by the Tolpuddle Farm Labour Information Centre, 1984.

8. Résumé and free translation from Michel Morisset, "Éléments pour une analyse matérialiste de l'agriculture au Québec," *Les Cahiers du Socialisme* (winter/spring 1981).

9. Morisset, "Éléments pour une analyse matérialiste de l'agriculture au Québec."

10. Michel Morisset, "De la famille à la compagnie, le travail reste ardu et dangereux," *Le Devoir*, vol. LXXV, no. 275, section C3 (November 26, 1984), p. 2.

11. Smith, "Not Enough Hours, Our Accountant Tells Me'," p. 6.

12. *Ibid.*, p. 11.

13. Stultz, taped interview.

14. Raj Chouhan, President, Canadian Farmworkers Union, Suite 1, 4725 Kingsway, Burnaby, British

Columbia, taped interview, December 1985.

15. Holt, "Introduction to the Seasonal Farm Labour Problem," p. 10.

16. Carolyn Sachs, "Women's Work in the U.S.: Variations by Region," *Agriculture and Human Values*, vol. 2, no. 1 (winter 1985), p. 37.

17. Stultz, taped interview.

18. Canada, Labour Canada, Federal-Provincial Relations Branch, *Minimum Wage Rates in Canada* (Ottawa: April 30, 1985), p. 2.

19. *Canada Labour Code*, R.S.C. 1970, c. L-1, as amended.

20. Mutale Chanda, former Canadian Farmworker's Union (Ontario) organizer, from video interview in *To Pick Is Not To Choose*.

21. William Yates Reno, "Why no legal rights for farm workers," *Canadian Labour* (November 30, 1979), p. 12.

22. The labour contractor situation in British Columbia, as reported to the author by Raj Chouhan of the CFU, is a very troublesome one. Contractors guarantee the grower with a steady group of workers. The labour contractor transports these workers (often in very unsafe and crowded vehicles), to and from the farm worksite each day. The grower turns over the collective wages to the contractor who is responsible for paying the worker. However, most often, the contractor pays the workers less than the established wage. Thus, the contractor keeps his "contractor's fee" on top of an unfair chunk of the farmworker's wages.

23. Farm Safety Association, *Ontario farm injury and fatality facts and figures: 10 year summary of Ontario Agricultural lost-time injuries* (Guelph, Ontario: 1984).

24. Ontario Task Force on Health and Safety in Agriculture, *Report* (Toronto: Ministry of Agriculture and Food; Ministry of Labour, 1985), pp. 23-24.

25. *An Act Respecting Labour Standards*, 1979, C-45, Regulation Respecting Labour Standards, O.C. 873-8L.

26. *Labour Standards Act*, the Labour Standards Regulation, S. Reg. 317/77, as amended.

27. *Employment Standards Act*, S.B.C., 1980 c. 10, as amended.

28. *Employment Standards Act*, O. Reg. 284/80, as amended.

29. Chouhan, taped interview.

30. Ingolf Vogeler, *The Myth of the Family Farm* (Boulder, Colorado: Westview Press, 1981), pp. 198-204.

31. "Micheline" and "Jeanne" interviews conducted and translated by Somer Brodbribb with two Quebec migrant farmworkers. Assumed names have been used in this article in order to protect these women from the consequences of speaking out. Without any legislative protection these women can be fired without any kind of legal recourse. At this point, the author would like to commend these farmworkers for their courage in telling their stories, and express her admiration for their dedication to, and caring for, Canada's national heritage of woodlands. The interviews were conducted in December 1985.

32. *Ibid.*

33. *Ibid.*

34. *Ibid.*

35. *Ibid.*

36. Ontario Task Force on Health and Safety in Agriculture, *Report*.

37. Stultz, taped interview.

38. "Micheline" and "Jeanne" interviews.

39. *Ibid.*

40. Chouhan, taped interview.

41. *Ibid.*

42. British Columbia Coroner's Office, Verdict of Coroner's Jury into the October 30, 1982 death of Jarnail Singh Deol in Surrey, British Columbia, pursuant to the *Coroners Act*, RSBC, March 11, 1983.

43. Susan Hundertmark, "Rural Feminism," *Healthsharing*, vol. 7, no. 1 (winter 1985), p. 14.

44. J.F. Castrilli and T. Vigod, "Pesticides: An Examination of Canadian Law and Policy," written for the Law Reform Commission of Canada, 1984.

45. Castrilli and Vigod, "Pesticides."

46. "Micheline" and "Jeanne" interviews.

47. Chouhan, taped interview.

48. Harasim, and Teles, *Farm Workers: The Invisible Minority in Ontario: an Introduction for the Public*, p. 2.

49. "Micheline" and "Jeanne" interviews.

50. *Ibid.*

51. *Ibid.*

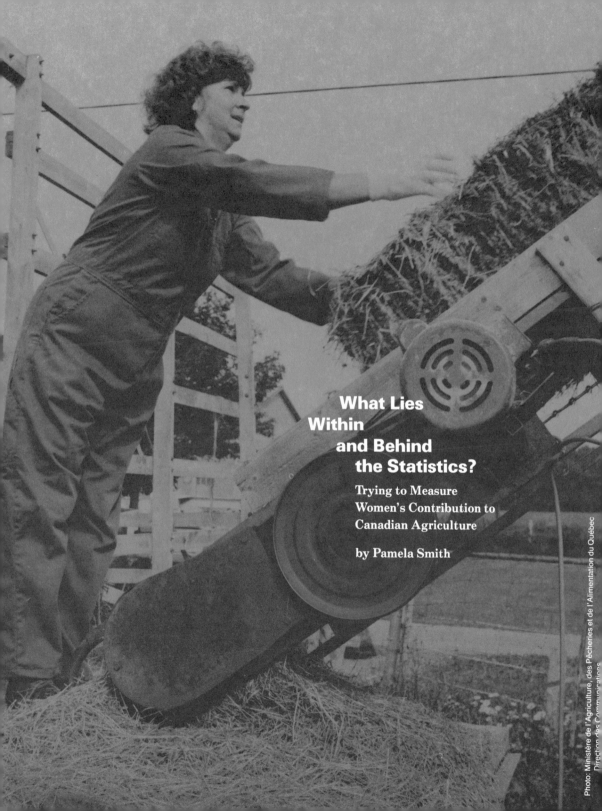

What Lies Within and Behind the Statistics?

Trying to Measure Women's Contribution to Canadian Agriculture

by Pamela Smith

4 TABLE OF CONTENTS

LIST OF FIGURES

LIST OF APPENDICES

LIST OF TABLES

127

**Trying to
measure
women's
contribution
to Canadian
agriculture**

ACKNOWLEDGEMENTS

Doug Scott's and Elaine Wood's sensitive attention to detail is appreciated: they spent hours on the phone encouraging officers of farm organizations to participate in the survey and talking to deans or registrars of agriculture faculties or colleges. At Statistics Canada, Brenda Clarke (Agriculture Statistics Division), Tom Bird (Education Division), and Francine Monette (Labour and Household Surveys Division) responded to requests with promptness and courtesy.

Criticisms of earlier drafts improved this chapter; Ray D. Bollman, Alfred Cho Chung-Hing, and Marion Meredith are thanked for their assistance. Under less than ideal conditions, Janet O'Brien made the many changes which resulted in the final version of this article. The Library and Faculty of Graduate Studies and Research at the University of Regina are thanked again for their support.

This paper is offered to family and friends and to researchers in agriculture and/or women's work, and most especially to women and men on Canadian farms. We have attempted to reflect faithfully their work and experience. Errors in fact or of interpretation remain our responsibility.

Pamela Smith

INTRODUCTION

"We are farmers," Jeanne emphasized, ". . . definitely not farmerettes."[1]
Women's agricultural labour has long been one of the hidden costs of food
production in Canada. Many farm wives work without pay to do tasks on
the farm that would have to be paid for if labour were hired. Women's
work on the farm is treated as a natural extension of all women's work in
the home, and "therefore" has no particular economic value and deserves
no specific recognition (as tragically pointed out in the well-known
Murdoch case, among others). Significant financial contributions made
by women to family farming through income earned off the farm are
equally ignored even though: "It is becoming increasingly difficult for
many families to survive on the income generated by the farm operation
alone."[2]

Agriculture in Canada is generally regarded as a male domain.
Farmers and farm labourers are commonly assumed to be male.[3] There is
a tendency to characterize men's work in farming "specifically in terms of
their productive input to the agricultural enterprise; that of women is
described in terms of their activity in the domestic unit."[4] Women's work
in primary agriculture has therefore been overlooked or minimized. Thus,
in Canada, as in other countries, exploration of the actual amount, type,
and extent of women's contribution to agriculture has only just begun. It
is a complex task.

Most primary agricultural production in Canada is based on family
farms, where most or all of the labour required to operate the farm is
provided by members of the family, which owns the other necessary
resources: land and equipment. Legal title to the land, however, has
traditionally been held by the male adults in the family; thus, *operators* of
the farm are assumed to be men. Most studies suggest that, in farming,
there is a rigid division of labour according to sex: men are assumed to be
involved in primary agricultural production, and women are seen to
contribute (if at all) with *ancillary* services, such as cooking for crews of
threshers or harvesters.

Whatever the historical basis for these concepts, women's work on

the farm is changing, and changing dramatically. Evolution of the
Canadian family farm has had profound implications for the work of
women on farms. The small mixed family farm of 50 years ago has nearly
disappeared. Agricultural production has become increasingly large-
scale, mechanized, and specialized, and much more capital-intensive. At
least some of the work traditionally done by farm women is no longer
done on the farm. One woman recounts the changes in her work over the
past 20 years:

131

**Trying to
measure
women's
contribution
to Canadian
agriculture**

> Well, I used to do a lot of milking, and I used to feed the calves. And we had
> hens that had to be cleaned out periodically and fed. I used to have to clean
> out the pigs too, but not very often . . . But our methods of farming have
> changed. In the past few years, we have only had beef cattle. We have smaller
> cattle in the barn at the other place, and my husband finishes cattle here at
> this barn. So, he can pretty well look after things himself.[5]

Many of the activities that were traditionally performed by farm
women, such as chicken-plucking, egg-candling, or cream-separating,
have moved off the farm and are now part of commercial food processing
in the *off-farm* labour market.

But more recently, women's work on the farm also has been changing
because women are moving into areas that traditionally have been
considered *men's work*. For example, more and more women are working
as paid farm labourers; and many more women are operating their own
farms. Women are also contributing financially to the farm enterprise
through income earned in off-farm employment. And, despite their
increased involvement in other types of work, women on farms, like
women in cities, continue to be responsible for the so-called *invisible* work
of homemaking. It is difficult, therefore, to measure women's contribution to agriculture.

For one thing, women who participate in Canadian agriculture are a
diverse group. For example, some of them come from families where
farming has been a way of life for many generations; others have only
recently become involved in farming. Farms themselves vary. Some
farms are large, and some are small; they may be heavily specialized in a
single commodity, or produce a variety of products; they may be
relatively debt-free, or deeply in debt. They may be situated in very
different geographical locations: some farms are close to large urban
centres and employment opportunities; others are several hours' drive

from a community with more than a vacant school and a closed post office.

The second element that makes it difficult to measure women's contribution to agriculture is a less obvious, and, perhaps, more fundamental difference among women on farms: women's relationship to the farm family, and to the farm itself. For example, some women own and operate their own farms. Others are wives, daughters, or relatives of farm owners or operators. Still others have no family relationship to the farm, but are involved as paid employees in agricultural work. All of these women contribute to Canadian agriculture, but under quite different terms and conditions, and at widely varying rates of reward for their efforts.

What is the nature of their contribution? Defining this term is also difficult and is the third reason that "measuring" women's contribution is a complex issue. Women are directly and visibly involved in agriculture through their work in fields and barns; they may also keep accounts and records for the farm. But women contribute as well when they work off the farm at other occupations to provide a source of income that may assist the farm and improve the living standard of the farm family. Women contribute further through their homemaking, as they raise, support, and nurture family members on the farm. Not all women on all Canadian farms engage in all of these activities, however. One activity may predominate over the others, depending on the life cycle of the woman and her family, and the nature of the farm itself.

Because there is little social recognition of their work, women on farms have been organizing and successfully making their voices heard in the farm community and beyond. However, to lobby requires a good deal of documentation. Awareness of the status quo is not enough, these women have discovered. Evidence must be presented in a manner that convinces others, especially policy-makers, bureaucrats, and governments. Therefore, women have begun to gather data describing their contribution to agriculture. They have documented the numbers of women who work off the farm and how much money they return to the farm enterprise; the risks to women's and children's health and safety brought by work on the farm; the stress experienced by women as they try to keep farm families and family farming together; the effects of certain policies on farm women; the needs of women for training, education, support, and services; and many more aspects of their experience. (See the bibliography.) Ground-breaking studies in a particular region or province have been carried out, revealing some striking common issues about women's involvement in farm work and about their needs.

Policy-makers use national figures to monitor trends in Canada, basing their political and economic decisions, in part, on these figures. But national statistics on agriculture have tended to be gender-blind, and have been presented in a manner that makes it difficult to determine or to document women's specific role and contribution to Canadian agriculture. Thus, women's enormous contribution to family farms and, therefore, to the backbone of Canadian agriculture is frequently ignored by politicians, policy-makers, and by the statisticians and economists who measure and quantify inputs to Canadian agriculture.

Failure to count women in the national figures contributes to their invisibility. But much information *exists*: the problem is to gain access to it and to interpret it to reveal women's work in agriculture.

By using national statistics, for example, it is possible to estimate how many hours farm women work at off-farm jobs, or how many hours they work as unpaid farm labourers on family farms. It is possible to identify the different contributions made by women to different types of commodity production, and to ascertain the numbers of women operating certain types of farms. Armed with these figures, women will be better prepared to analyse the effect of certain policies on family farms and on the women who live on family farms. The figures can also be used to substantiate claims that farm women are making *for recognition as essential participants* in all forms of agricultural work in this country.

This article endeavours to add to the quest of farm women for equality by analysing national statistical information and illustrating women's formidable and growing contribution to Canadian family farms today. It is hoped that women will be able to use this information in their own discussions and analyses, and in their lobby for changes to agricultural policy that will take women's contribution into central consideration. The article presents a statistical profile of women in three areas of agricultural activity: their contribution to family farming; their participation in agricultural organizations; and their involvement in agricultural education. The main emphasis, however, is on documenting women's work on family farms, including their work on the farm, off the farm, and in the home. The article examines women's work as an agricultural work force over the past 65 years; women's involvement in family farms; demographic characteristics of women on Canadian family farms; social factors affecting women's contribution to family farms; the nature of women's work in family agriculture, on and off the farm; the relationship between women's contribution and farm type; and the presence of women in agricultural education and farm organizations.

Estimates of women's contribution presented in this article depend largely upon the 1981 Census. There are limitations in using census figures (discussed more fully in Appendix A). Admittedly, these estimates do not provide a complete picture of the scope and variety of women's contribution. However, they are a useful starting point.

Although the 1986 Census was the most recent, it was a partial census and its results are not yet available in a form that can be analysed. In light of the escalating farm financial crisis, it may be that the 1986 figures will reveal an even greater economic contribution by women to the family farm. It is hoped, therefore, that this article will also serve as a model for the type of questions that women can ask from the national statistics in 1986 and in future years.

How can the extent of women's involvement in agriculture be measured on a national basis? One starting point is to simply count how many women work in this sector of the economy. The three national sources of information are the population census for each decade; the agricultural census (which can be used in conjunction with the population census); and the monthly Labour Force Survey, from which annual estimates are made.

Counting women in agriculture, however, is not a straightforward task. For reasons inherent in the method by which national data are collected and classified, many women who contribute to Canadian agriculture may be excluded from the estimates. Because only one occupation is listed for an individual, a woman who works on the farm, as well as holding a secretarial job, for example, in a nearby town, may be most likely to report her off-farm clerical work. Although she may spend almost as many hours in the fields, the census form does not permit her to report her primary agricultural work, or to be included in national estimates of the agricultural work force. (This problem also applies to men on farms who also work off-farm.) Another problem arises when attributing meaning to the various census categories. For example, the census uses the category *farm operator*. Only one operator is identified for each farm — the person who makes the day-to-day decisions. In practice, however, this category may not reflect the person who actually works the farm, or show who really participates in the decision-making process for each farm family.

Nevertheless, the national data are an important means of discovering national trends. They also reveal how women's involvement in agriculture has changed over time. The rate of change of women's work in agriculture since 1921 is examined in the next section.

Sixty-Five Years of Women's Work in Agriculture

Whether as farmers, labourers, or managers and foremen, Canadian women have become increasingly involved in primary agriculture over the past 65 years. In 1921, slightly less than 2% of the Canadian agricultural labour force was female. By 1981, one in five persons reporting an agricultural occupation was a woman. No other single major occupational group recorded as great a change in its composition by sex between 1921 and 1971[6]. As shown in Figure 1, most of this growth occurred after World War II. While in 1951 there were only 32,567 women with an agricultural occupation (4% of the agricultural work force), by 1981, over 21% (107,560) of the agricultural work force was female.

**Figure 1: Women as percentage of agricultural work force,
Canada, 1951-1981**

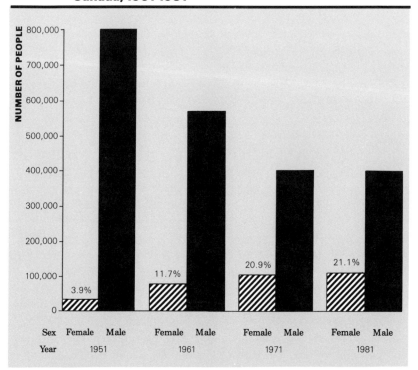

Source: Canada, Dominion Bureau of Statistics and Statistics Canada, Census, *Labour Force Series*, 1951-1981.

This increase is even more dramatic when it is considered that the size of the Canadian agricultural labour force has been decreasing steadily, from 797,874 in 1951 to 508,700 in 1981. Furthermore, although many women who were unpaid family workers were excluded from the 1971 estimates, the number of women with agricultural occupations remained high in that year, suggesting that women became more involved in *both* paid and unpaid capacities in agricultural work.

137

Trying to
measure
women's
contribution
to Canadian
agriculture

What exactly do these figures represent? Are women indeed becoming more active in Canadian agriculture? If so, how?

National census data provide two ways to assess women's direct involvement in agriculture: in terms of their *occupational title* and their *class of worker* status.

■ Occupational title

The census recognizes four types of agricultural occupations: farmer, labourer, manager/foreman, and other. Although the percentage of women in all these occupations has grown, the greatest actual increase was in the labourer category. Furthermore, although there are fewer farmers than there were 30 years ago, more of them are female.

Table 1 illustrates these changes. In 1951, for example, 830,441 people reported an agricultural occupation; 66% of these were farmers. By 1981, only 44% were farmers. Only 1.5% (8,092) of farmers were female in 1951; whereas in 1981, almost 9% (19,610) of farmers were women. In contrast, the proportion of the agricultural labour force that was farm labourers remained constant during this period, at approximately 32%. The percentage of *women farm labourers*, however, increased dramatically over a 30-year period: from 9% in 1951 to 43% by 1981. Women's participation has also increased in the other agricultural occupations.[7]

■ Class of worker

Census data also differentiate between three different classes of worker: unpaid family worker; wage earner; and self-employed. Over the past 30 years, the proportion of women in all classes of agricultural worker has increased. Although the self-employed category displayed the greatest rate of increase, self-employed women remain a relatively small group in the agricultural work force. Women's participation in both paid and unpaid categories is increasing at similar rates, with the result that *two-thirds* of unpaid family workers and almost one-quarter of paid workers in Canadian agriculture are women.

Table 2 illustrates changing patterns in women's agricultural

Table 1: Individuals with an agricultural occupation, by sex and occupational title, Canada, 1951-1981

OCCUPATIONAL TITLE

Sex/Year	Farmers number	% of total	Farm Managers and Foremen* number	% of total	Farm Labourers number	% of total	Nursery Workers Gardeners and Ground Keepers number	% of total	Other* number	% of total	Total number	%
Males												
1951	536,929	67.3	3,816	0.5	238,598	29.9	2,183	0.3	16,348	2.0	797,874	100
1961	384,410	67.1	3,242	0.6	156,250	27.3	24,411	4.3	4,785	0.8	573,098	100
1971	226,335	55.8	22,945	5.7	113,410	28.0	37,620	9.3	4,990	1.2	405,300	100
1981***	206,515	51.5	37,825	9.4	92,305	23.0	55,100	13.7	9,385	2.3	401,130	100
Females												
1951	8,092	24.8	90	0.3	23,844	73.2	71	0.2	470	1.4	32,567	100
1961	8,996	11.8	101	0.1	66,081	87.1	329	0.4	361	0.5	75,868	100
1971	7,680	7.2	1,075	1.0	96,015	89.9	1,690	1.6	390	0.4	106,850	100
1981***	19,610	18.2	6,575	6.1	69,120	64.3	10,790	10.0	1,470	1.4	107,560	100
Total												
1951	545,021	65.6	3,906	0.5	262,442	31.6	2,254	0.3	16,818	2.0	830,441	100
1961	393,406	60.6	3,343	0.5	222,331	34.3	24,740	3.8	5,146	0.8	648,966	100
1971	234,015	45.7	24,020	4.7	209,425	40.9	39,310	7.7	5,380	1.1	512,150	100
1981***	226,125	44.5	44,400	8.7	161,425	31.7	65,885	13.0	10,855	2.1	508,690	100
Females as per cent of total												
1951		1.5		2.3		9.1		3.1		2.8		3.9
1961		2.3		3.0		29.7		1.3		7.0		11.7
1971		3.3		4.5		45.8		4.3		7.2		20.9
1981		8.7		14.8		42.8		16.4		13.5		21.1

Source: Canada, Dominion Bureau of Statistics, 1951 Census of Population, *Labour Force*, vol. IV, table 11; Canada, Dominion Bureau of Statistics, 1961 Census of Population, *Labour Force*, vol. III, table 20; Canada, Statistics Canada, 1971 Census of Population, *Labour Force*, vol. III, table 8; Canada, Statistics Canada, 1981 Census of Population, *Labour Force Occupation Trends*, table 1.

Notes: * For 1951 and 1961, this title is unspecified. In 1971 and 1981, it includes only machinery operators and custom workers; remaining "others" for these years have been included with farm labourers.

** Figures reported here include farm managers who are not included in the agricultural occupations classification in 1981, but some of whom are reported under management (1,146). They are based on 1971 SOC codes, in order to preserve comparability.

Table 2: Individuals with an agricultural occupation, by sex and class of worker, Canada, 1951-1981

| | CLASS OF WORKER | | | | | | | |
| | Self-Employed* | | Wage Earner* | | Unpaid Family Worker | | Total | |
Sex/Year	number	% of total	number	% of total	number	% of total	number	% of total
Males								
1951	536,872	67.5	131,701	16.6	126,301	15.9	794,874	100
1961	387,442	67.6	117,287	20.5	68,369	11.9	573,098	100
1971	229,065	56.5	131,835	32.5	44,400**	11.0	405,300	100
1981***	219,155	54.6	168,190	41.9	13,785**	3.4	401,130	100
Females								
1951	8,186	25.1	6,215	19.1	18,166	55.8	32,567	100
1961	9,074	12.0	10,245	13.5	56,549	74.5	75,868	100
1971	7,875	7.4	27,030	25.3	71,945**	67.3	106,850	100
1981***	25,730	23.9	53,060	49.3	28,775**	26.8	107,565	100
Total								
1951	545,058	65.6	137,916	16.6	144,467	17.4	827,441	100
1961	396,516	61.1	127,532	19.7	124,918	19.2	648,966	100
1971	236,940	46.3	158,865	31.0	116,345**	22.7	512,150	100
1981***	244,885	48.1	221,250	43.5	42,560**	8.4	508,695	100
Females as % total								
1951		1.5		4.5		12.6		3.9
1961		2.3		8.0		45.3		11.7
1971		3.3		17.0		61.8		20.9
1981		10.5		24.0		67.6		21.1

Source: Canada, Dominion Bureau of Statistics, 1951 Census of Population, *Labour Force*, vol. IV, table 11; Canada, Dominion Bureau of Statistics, 1961 Census of Population, *Labour Force*, vol. III, table 20; Canada, Statistics Canada, 1971 Census of Population, *Labour Force*, vol. III, table 8; Canada, Statistics Canada, 1981 Census of Population, unpublished tabulations.

Notes: *Self-employed individuals in incorporated companies are classified as wage earners in 1971 and 1981.

　　　　　**The number of unpaid family workers is higher in 1971 and lower in 1981 compared to other censuses because of the way the questions were asked. See: Gilles Simard, "Analyse du statut professionel et de la forme juridique au Recensement de 1981," unpublished paper, Statistics Canada, February 1984.

　　　　　***Figures reported here include farm managers who are not included in the agricultural occupations classification in 1981, but some of whom are reported under management (1,146). They are based on 1971 SOC codes, in order to preserve comparability.

participation in relation to class of worker, based on the censuses since 1951.

Among the three classes of workers, women are most heavily represented in the unpaid family worker category. Women's involvement here has increased dramatically, from 13% in 1951, to 68% in 1981. In 1951, women represented less than 5% of the paid agricultural labour force; by 1981, this proportion had increased to 24%. The percentage of self-employed women increased tenfold: from 1% in 1951 to 10% in 1981.

Analysis of the annual summaries of the Labour Force Survey between 1975 and 1983 reveals the same general trend: women's participation in the agricultural industry is increasing, even though the size of the agricultural labour force is diminishing. As illustrated in Table 3, in 1975, women composed 22% of the total 483,000 workers in agriculture. By 1983, 29% of Canada's agricultural labour force consisting of 476,000 workers was female.

Table 3: Number and percentage of women as paid, unpaid, and self-employed agricultural workers, Canada, 1975 and 1983

Class of Worker	Number of persons (000s)* 1975		1983		Women as % of Class 1975	1983
	Women	Men	Women	Men		
unpaid family	62	30	55	23	67	70
paid worker	33	104	53	103	24	34
self-employed**	12	241	29	214	5	12
Total	107	375	137	340	22	29

Source: Canada, Statistics Canada, unpublished tabulations for the Labour Force Survey.

Notes: *Number of workers based on annual averages of monthly observations.

**Self-employed category includes those with and without employees.

■ Hours of work

The Labour Force Survey also provides information about hours of work of the agricultural labour force. This source shows that women are working more hours per week in agriculture today than they were a few years ago. Both the absolute number and the proportion of hours worked by women in agricultural occupations increased between 1975 and 1983.

As shown in Table 4, women worked 3,545,000 hours in the agricultural industry in 1975 (15% of all the hours reported). By 1983, women worked 20% (4,072,000) of all agricultural hours. Women in the unpaid family worker group contributed 1,543,000 of hours worked in 1983, which comprised two-thirds of the total weekly hours worked by unpaid family workers of both sexes.

Table 4: Women's weekly agricultural hours and women's hours as percentage of each class of agricultural worker, Canada, 1975 and 1983

| Class of Worker | Number of Hours per Week (000s)* | | | | Women's Hours as % of Class Hours | |
| | 1975 | | 1983 | | 1975 | 1983 |
	Women	Men	Women	Men		
unpaid family	1,953	1,265	1,543	776	61	67
paid worker	1,092	4,798	1,564	4,623	19	25
self-employed	500	14,030	965	11,249	3	8
Total	3,545	20,093	4,072	16,648	15	20

Source: Canada, Statistics Canada, unpublished tabulations from the Labour Force Survey.

Note: *Annual averages of 12 monthly surveys. Aggregate hours are reported in thousands (000s).

Women on Family Farms

Women are working in Canadian agriculture in many ways. Their increasing involvement as paid labourers in agribusiness and corporate farms is a significant trend, which is analysed in Julie Lee's article in this publication. As mentioned in the introduction, however, family farming is still the most prevalent mode of Canadian agricultural production: in 1981, 87% of all Canadian farms were family farms. As can be seen from the large percentage of women who work as unpaid family labourers, this sector of Canadian agriculture depends heavily on women's work. The following sections provide information about the family farm women, and about the ways they contribute to family farming — whether as operators or as wives of operators.

Who are the women living and working on Canadian family farms? Do the statistics confirm any of the popular assumptions about Canadian farm women?

Marital status

One common assumption is that the only women who run farms on their own are widows, that is, that women become operators only when they are forced to do so by their husbands' deaths. Census figures for 1981 reveal a different picture. As Table 5 shows, fully 60% of the 8,085 women operating Canadian family farms were married. Another 7% were separated or divorced, and 2% were single. The remaining 30% were, indeed, widows.

Table 5: Operators and spouses on family farms in economic families with one operator, by sex and marital status, Canada, 1981

| Marital Status | OPERATORS | | | | SPOUSES | | | |
| | Male | | Female | | Male | | Female | |
	N	%	N	%	N	%	N	%
married	258,820	95.8	4,860	60.1	4,775	100	260,510	100
separated/ divorced	1,695	0.6	555	6.9	not applicable			
widowed	1,530	0.6	2,465	30.5	not applicable			
single	8,045	3.0	205	2.5	not applicable			
Total	270,090	100	8,085	100	4,775	100	260,510	100

Source: Canada, Statistics Canada, unpublished tabulations from Agriculture Population Linkage, 1981 Censuses.

Note: Family farms include individual proprietorships, partnerships, and family corporations and excludes institutional, Hutterite, non-family corporations, and other farms and community pastures.

Economic families include two or more individuals living in the same dwelling, related to the census farm operator by birth, marriage, or adoption.

Families with more than one operator are excluded.

Notable increases between 1971 and 1981 have been reported in the proportion of married or divorced women operators.[8] This suggests a relatively new trend. The assumption that most women operators were widows may have been well-founded in the past but is now becoming outdated.

Education

Studies of limited samples of women living on farms have frequently noted that they are more likely to have completed higher levels of formal education than have their partners. Statistics Canada figures confirm these findings on a national basis. As shown in Table 6, however, the pattern is complex, and varies subtly, depending on whether the woman is an operator or the spouse of the operator.

Women operators are likely to have had more formal education than have male operators. Women operators also have somewhat higher levels of completed formal education than have female spouses. For example,

Table 6: Operators and spouses on family farms, by sex and education, Canada, 1981

Level of Education	OPERATORS				SPOUSES			
	Male		Female		Male		Female	
	N	%	N	%	N	%	N	%
less than Grade 9	94,280	34.9	2,060	25.5	1,175	24.6	58,410	22.4
grade 9-10	55,595	20.6	1,215	15.0	720	15.1	48,050	18.4
grade 11-13	48,860	18.1	1,755	21.7	865	18.1	68,650	26.4
other post-secondary	43,055	15.9	1,555	19.2	990	20.7	55,640	21.4
completed university	28,300	10.5	1,500	18.6	1,025	21.5	29,760	11.4
Total	270,090	100	8,085	100	4,775	100	260,510	100

Source: Canada, Statistics Canada, unpublished tabulations from Agriculture Population Linkage, 1981 Censuses.

Note: Family farms are economic families with only one operator.

19% of women operators completed university, compared to 10% of their
male counterparts and 11% of female spouses. Women who operate farms
are also twice as likely to have completed university than has the average
Canadian working woman; in 1981, only 9% of the female labour force had
completed university. This difference does not apply to men; 12% of men
in the labour force had completed university, compared to 10% of men
who operate farms.[9]

Age

Between 1971 and 1981, the average age of Canadian farmers dropped,
reversing a trend of continuous increase since the mid-1950s.[10] It has been
suggested, however, that female operators tend to be older than their
male counterparts.[11] Another study reported "dramatic differences" in
age between male and female operators in 1971,[12] and also found that the
rate of increase among women operators under age 45 was greater than
among men, a trend that would reduce such differences.

Age may now no longer distinguish female and male operators as
much as it has previously. As shown in Table 7, 1981 census figures

**Table 7: Operators and spouses on family farms, by sex
and age, Canada, 1981**

| Age | OPERATORS | | | | SPOUSES | | | |
| | Male | | Female | | Male | | Female | |
Categories	N	%	N	%	N	%	N	%
less than 25 years	6,655	2.5	185	2.3	45	0.9	13,405	5.2
25-34 years	49,280	18.2	1,395	17.3	940	19.7	59,545	22.9
35-44 years	64,835	24.0	2,010	24.9	1,320	27.6	67,760	26.0
45-64 years	124,770	46.2	3,660	45.2	1,950	40.8	106,505	40.9
65 years or more	24,550	9.1	835	10.3	520	10.9	13,295	5.1
Total	270,090	100	8,085	100	4,775	100	260,510	100

Source: Canada, Statistics Canada, unpublished tabulations from Agriculture Population
Linkage, 1981 Censuses.

revealed no noteworthy differences in age distribution of male and female operators.

Both female and male operators tend to concentrate in the 45-to-64-year age group. Wives of male operators tend to be somewhat younger than their partners (a common pattern in Canadian society) as are husbands of women operators.

Fertility

It is frequently assumed that farm women have larger families than urban women. On the other hand, it has also been suggested that women's increased involvement in agriculture has been caused by or has resulted from decreased fertility rates. Do women on farms have more children than do urban women? Is this pattern changing? The answer to both questions is *yes*. As shown in Table 8, women on farms have tended to bear, and continue to bear, more children than have women living in urban centres. However, the differences between the fertility rates of farm women and other women are diminishing.

Table 8: Number of children ever born to married women, by selected ages and urban size, Canada, 1981

| | Age Groups, In Years | | | | |
	25-29	30-34	35-39	55-59	70 or more
Urban sizes					
rural farm	1.8	2.4	2.9	4.2	4.6
all urban	1.2	1.9	2.2	3.1	3.1

Source: Canada, Statistics Canada, 1981 Census, *Population: Nuptiality and Fertility,* table 2, catalogue no. 92-906.

Rural farm women in the over-70 age group have had 1.5 more children than have their counterparts in urban areas. In the younger age groups, the difference is less pronounced; for example, rural women in the youngest age group (25 to 29) have had 1.8 children, compared to 1.2 children by their urban counterparts. Coupled with farm women's increasing on- and off-farm work, these findings are significant to the debate surrounding the need for child care in rural and farm areas. (For further discussion of this question, see Ginette Busque's article in this publication.)

Ethnicity
Are women from certain ethnic groups more likely to work on a farm? The history of immigration and migration in Canada is intimately linked to the history and development of Canadian farming. Regional variations in Canadian farming might be explained by the cultural and organizational practices of different ethnocultural groups. For example, cultural practices might influence division of labour on a farm, ownership patterns (such as the collective rather than individual use of land), or methods of cultivation. Nevertheless, statistics suggest there is no link between ethnicity and proportion of female operators in Canadian family farms.

■   What do the statistics tell us about women's work on family farms? As well as the basic demographic factors outlined above, national data sources can reveal a great deal more about women's work in family agriculture. The balance of this article will focus, therefore, on assessing the contribution of women who are members of a farm family,* that is, an economic family in which there is a farm operator. In this article, these women are referred to as *farm women.*

The question, then, changes from: "How do women contribute to Canadian agriculture?" to "What do data available from national sources tell us about the involvement of women in single-operator economic family farms?" The following sections address this question.

Farmers, daughters, and wives: women's position in farm families
In 1981, there were 318,361 Canadian farms with annual sales of more than $250.[13] Of these, 278,180 (87%) were operated by one person, who was also a member of an economic family. (Approximately one-third of the remaining 13% were multi-operator farms. Census figures do not provide

---

*In this article, farm families are defined in terms of the *economic family* unit. An economic family consists of the operator and anyone else related to her/him by marriage, common-law, blood, or adoption, living together in the same dwelling. This is a broader concept of *family* than is commonly used, and permits inclusion, for example, of the work of sisters, aunts, nieces, and grandmothers, as well as spouses and children.

a means to assess the degree of women's involvement in these.) In total, 351,120 women were associated with these farms. As illustrated in Figure 2, only 3% (8,085) were themselves farm operators. Wives of operators totalled 260,510, and were present in 94% of the farms. Another 82,525 were daughters and female relatives over 15 years of age; these were present on 30% of the farms.

Figure 2: Occupations of all women on family farms, Canada, 1981

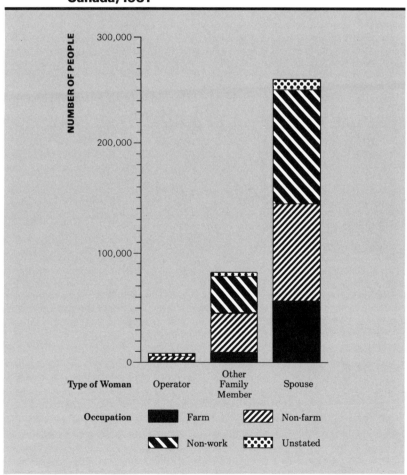

Source: Canada, Statistics Canada, unpublished tabulations from Agriculture Population Linkage, 1981 Censuses.

The occupations of these women varied. Some did not report an occupation; some were directly involved in primary agriculture; and a large proportion (well over a third) provided direct assistance to the farming operation through employment in non-agricultural occupations.

As shown in Table 9, women who operated their own farms usually worked in agricultural occupations: almost half of all the operators, compared to 22% of spouses and 11% of other female relatives, had their main occupation in agriculture. A large proportion of farm women worked in non-agricultural occupations: almost half of the other female relatives, and one-third of operators and spouses held jobs outside agriculture. Only one-quarter of female operators, compared to 44% of spouses and of other relatives, did not report an occupation.

Table 9: Occupations of women operators, spouses, and other relatives on family farms, Canada, 1981

	Agricultural Occupations (%)	Not Working or No occupation Stated (%)	Non-Agricultural Occupations (%)	TOTAL (%)
operators	42	25	33	100
spouses	22	44	34	100
daughters/other family members	11	44	45	100

Source: Special calculation from Statistics Canada, unpublished tabulations from Agriculture Population Linkage, 1981 Censuses.

These figures indicate a significant degree of agricultural involvement for all farm women. Nevertheless, it is likely that they underestimate women's agricultural work on family farms.

Statistics Canada does not accommodate *homemaker* as an occupation, unless the tasks associated with this job are performed outside one's own family, and for pay. Therefore, most women who contribute in an important way to the farm family, through housework and homemaking support, would be included in the *no occupation* group. Many of these women may, in fact, be directly involved in agricultural labour at certain times of the year. For some, the distinction between *housework* and *farm work* may be unclear or unperceived. In addition, they may consider their work as unpaid family workers not worth reporting.

Another potential source of underestimation arises for the farm women working off-farm in non-agricultural occupations as well as on the farm. The census permits the listing of only one main occupation. (See Appendix A for discussion of limitations in using national data sources.)

The actual extent of women's contribution to family farming is difficult to estimate without carefully analysing hours and type of work. The following sections examine women's contribution in more detail.

How many farm women work in agriculture?
Seventeen per cent (60,550) of the 351,120 women living and working on Canadian family farms in 1981 were members of economic family/single-operator farms *and* reported having worked in agricultural occupations during the last week of May 1981. These women can unequivocally be considered directly involved in agriculture.

As already mentioned, these estimates are conservative, since they exclude secondary or additional occupations. As well, both an agricultural occupation *and* hours of work must be reported. Accordingly, the figure 60,550 represents the minimum number of women who directly contribute to Canadian agriculture. As shown in Table 10, most of these women (85%) were spouses of operators; 5% were operators themselves and 10% were other family members. The statistics also show additional important differences between the reported hours of women who are operators and those who are spouses of operators.

Women who operate their own farms are very visible in their direct involvement in agriculture. Table 10 shows that 36% reported some hours of work in May 1981. Most (87%) of these women were self-employed and 12% were paid workers.

Women classified as spouses of operators were much less likely to have an agricultural occupation, and almost half of those who did were unpaid. Table 10 shows that almost 20% of farm women reported some hours of work; 23,810 (46%) were classified as unpaid family workers. A little over one-third, however, were self-employed in agriculture, and 17% received a wage or salary.

Relatively few other female family members were employed in agriculture, and even fewer reported hours of work. On the other hand, those who did work in agriculture were usually paid for their work. Table 10 also shows that other female family members were much more likely than were spouses to be paid for their agricultural work. (Sixty per cent were reported as paid workers.) On the whole, then, almost half of all family farm women working directly in agriculture did so without pay.

Working for free on the family farm: paid and unpaid agricultural labour
The total number of hours that women on family farms spend working in

Table 10: All women on family farms and women reporting hours in agriculture, by relationship to operator and class of work, Canada, 1981

	ALL WOMEN ON FAMILY FARMS		WOMEN WITH HOURS IN AGRICULTURE*				
	N	%		N	% of total	% within class	% of "all women"
Operators	8,085	2.3	**Operators**	2,915	4.8	100	36.1
			self-employed	2,520		86.5	
			paid	360		12.3	
			unpaid	35		1.2	
Spouses	260,510	74.2	**Spouses**	51,340	84.8	100	19.7
			self-employed	18,750		36.5	
			paid	8,780		17.1	
			unpaid	23,810		46.4	
Other Female Family Members	82,525	23.5	**Other Female Family Members**	6,295	10.4	100	7.6
			self-employed	220		3.5	
			paid	3,790		60.2	
			unpaid	2,285		36.3	
Total	351,120	100	**Total**	60,550	100	100	17.2
			self-employed	21,490		35.5	
			paid	12,930		21.3	
			unpaid	26,130		43.2	

Source: Canada, Statistics Canada, unpublished tabulations from Agriculture Population Linkage, 1981 Censuses.

Note: *All those who had no occupation stated, even if they had hours, and those who were reported as employed in agriculture, but had no hours, have been excluded.

agricultural occupations is another measure in assessing women's agricultural labour. When all of the hours spent on agricultural work by farm family members are considered, the picture in Figure 3 emerges.

Figure 3: Aggregate hours in agriculture by sex, class of on-farm worker, and family membership, Canada, 1981

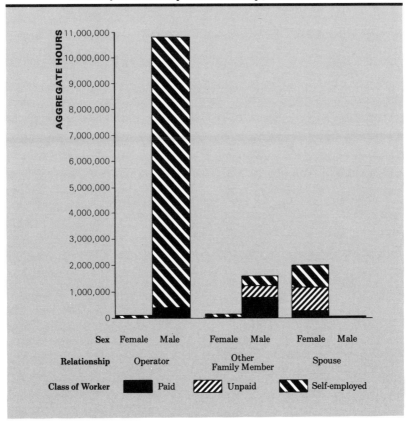

Source: Canada, Statistics Canada, unpublished tabulations from Agriculture Population Linkage, 1981 Censuses.

It is estimated that a total of 14.8 million hours of agricultural work were done in Canadian family farms in the last week of May 1981. Male operators worked 10.8 million hours in that week; female spouses worked 1.9 million hours; other male family members, 1.6 million hours; and other female family members, 1.75 thousand hours.[14] In total, women contributed 15% of all agricultural hours worked on family farms, or approximately 2.2 million hours. It should be noted that this figure represents the most conservative estimate of the number of hours that women contributed to family agriculture.

Overall, only 21% of women on family farms were paid for their hours of farm work. As shown in Table 10, almost half (43%) of all the women working on family farms did so as unpaid family labourers. The remaining 36% of women with agricultural hours were self-employed. Another source confirms these estimates: a survey of women members of the National Farmer's Union also found that only 21% of women received a wage for their farm work.[15]

Within the labour force as a whole, women (2.4%) are more likely than men (0.4%) to be employed as unpaid family workers.[16] These differences are especially profound in the agricultural sector where "nearly half (49%) of the women employed in agriculture were unpaid family workers, compared with only 7% of their male counterparts," according to Labour Canada figures for 1981.[17]

Similarly, the findings illustrated in Figure 3 point to an obvious link between the sex of the family member and unpaid, versus self-employed or paid, hours. For example, 66% of the 1.3 million unpaid family hours were worked by wives of operators. As well, although other female relatives were least likely to be directly involved in agricultural work, they were more likely to work without pay than were male relatives: 31% of women relatives were unpaid family labourers, compared to 24% of their male counterparts.

Women's hours of work on family farms

It is generally assumed that farmers work long hours. What is the situation for women farmers and for women involved in agriculture? In 1981, women in the Canadian labour force worked an average of 29.3 hours in the reference week, compared to 37.5 hours worked by men.[18] In the same week, women directly involved in agriculture worked an average of 37 hours. Many farm women worked even longer hours. Self-employed female spouses, for example, worked an average of 41 hours in agriculture, as shown in Table 11.

Table 11 shows that female operators worked about 39 hours per week, contributing about 5% of the total women's hours worked in agriculture on family farms. Female spouses worked an average of 38

153

Trying to
measure
women's
contribution
to Canadian
agriculture

Table 11: **Average hours of work per week and total weekly hours, by relationship to operator and class of work, of all women on family farms in economic families with only one operator, reporting hours in agriculture, Canada, 1981**

Women With Hours in Agriculture	Women		Average Hours/ Week	Total Weekly Hours	% of total	% within type
	N	%				
Operators	2,915	4.8	39	113,140	5.1	100
self-employed	2,520		40	100,865		89.2
paid	360		31	11,015		9.7
unpaid	35		36	1,260		1.1
Spouses	51,340	84.8	38	1,942,650	86.9	100
self-employed	18,750		41	768,845		39.6
paid	8,780		36	317,360		16.3
unpaid	23,810		36	856,445		44.1
Other Female Family Members	6,295	10.4	28	179,010	8.0	100
self-employed	220		49	11,070		6.2
paid	3,790		29	111,255		62.1
unpaid	2,285		24	56,685		31.7
Total	60,550	100	37	2,234,800	100	100
self-employed	21,490		41	880,780		39.4
paid	12,930		34	439,630		19.7
unpaid	26,130		35	914,390		40.9

Source: Canada, Statistics Canada, unpublished tabulations from Agriculture Population Linkage, 1981 Censuses.

hours a week. They contributed 87% of the total hours worked by women in agriculture. A large percentage (44%) of their hours were unpaid. Almost another 40% of the spouses' hours were self-employed; women in this group worked an average of 41 hours per week. The remaining 16% of spouses' hours were paid.

As with the total numbers of women involved directly in agriculture, the hours that women work are also likely to be considerably underestimated. Wives of operators are unlikely to report an agricultural occupation, as mentioned above. But this does not mean that many do not perform agricultural tasks, as evidenced by several studies and reports from women's organizations. Furthermore, it should be noted that the hours spent by women on tasks considered to be their proper sphere (housework, homemaking, child care, food preparation, family accounting, gardening, etc.) do not generally enter into the estimates of women's agricultural work hours. Nevertheless, some of these may well include tasks that would be reported as agricultural if performed by someone else.

Therefore, it must be emphasized that the figure of approximately two million women's hours previously mentioned should be understood to represent the *minimum* number of hours contributed by women.

WOMEN'S ESSENTIAL CONTRIBUTION TO FAMILY FARMING

Several models are used in the literature to describe the different *types* of women involved in family farms. (Appendix B contains a fuller discussion of four such models.) These are commonly based on one fundamental distinction: whether women work on the farm or in the home. It has been argued that both types of work contribute to the economic life of the farm.[19] Nevertheless, the distinction remains important. The various modifications present only refinements to these two terms. However, some important omissions (such as lack of recognition of women's employment off the farm) mean that these types of models do not account for the full spectrum of women's contribution to agriculture.

As an alternative to other models, the author suggests using the terms *direct involvement, indirect support*, and *direct assistance* to describe various aspects of women's contribution to family agriculture. These are useful because they not only recognize women's contribution both on and off the farm, but also permit distinction between the two types of on-farm work.

Direct involvement describes women's work on the farm including field and barn work, as well as support, service, and management activities.

However, women also do work that is essential to the maintenance of the farm activities and indirectly supports agriculture, that is, the work in the home. *Indirect support* is used to describe women's household work. The term does not imply that household work is less important. Rather, because this work is not specifically done for agriculture as an industry, it is termed *indirect*. It should also be noted that, as there are no national data sources for household work, the extent of this *indirect support* cannot be clearly assessed at this time.

Direct assistance accounts for the income-generating work done by women off the farm. Income from such work, which is invested in the farm enterprise or goes to support the farm family, *directly assists* primary agriculture.

The three types of contribution are discussed separately below, based on information provided by regional studies, field work, surveys, and reports prepared by farm women themselves, to illustrate and complement the national data. A fuller and more detailed picture of the work that women actually do on family farms is thereby provided.

Direct Involvement (Women's Work on the Farm)

■ Field and barn work

Some researchers suggest that farm women are greatly involved in farm work.[20] National surveys found that 20% of farm women are regularly involved in barn and field work, and another 20% execute these tasks occasionally.[21] There are, however, some regional variations. One report examined women's participation in six important farm activities (field work with machinery, application of chemicals, harvesting, care of livestock, barn chores, and veterinary work) in Ontario and Prince Edward Island. Thirty-three per cent of Ontario farm women and 20% of farm women in Prince Edward Island were involved in these activities on a regular basis. Inclusion of those who did these tasks occasionally raises the figures to 40% and 41% respectively.[22]

A 1983 Quebec study found that women spent, on average, an hour and 20 minutes a day in activities more directly related to agricultural production, such as field and barn work, compared to just under five hours a day spent by men. Women's work, therefore, accounted for 27% of the total hours spent on these activities.[23]

■ Farm support, management, and service work

In addition to field and barn work, women's direct farm work includes essential tasks called farm support and farm service activities. These may include supervising family workers and hired labour, collecting information used in farm decisions, promoting and marketing farm products, and picking up parts and supplies. There are also management tasks, such as keeping farm production records and accounts, paying bills, preparing income tax forms, and answering the telephone. Routine management activities, such as bookkeeping and paying bills, account for a large portion of this work.[24]

Reports suggest that about 29% of farm women perform farm support and service activities on a regular basis, and an additional 18% do so occasionally. Approximately 86% of all farm women indicate that they maintain the farm books and records.[25] The Quebec study already

mentioned found that 32% of farm women were sole keepers of the farm
books, and another 19% performed this task with their partners.[26]

Indirect Support (Women's Work in the Home)

Whether on the farm or in the city, household work tends to remain women's primary responsibility. In fact, it remains a woman's responsibility even when she works for pay outside the home, thereby creating a double workday situation for most women in Canada.[27] In farm families, as in most other Canadian families,

> ...the fact that household tasks are taken for granted as women's responsibilities and not shared responsibilities of both husband and wife, means that many other tasks which the woman assumes are added on to her original workload in the household.[28]

It has been estimated that, depending on whether they work outside the home, Canadian women spend between 30 and 39 hours per week on homemaking activities.[29] One American study suggests that *farm women* spend even more time in household work than do urban women.[30]

Recent studies of provincial and regional groups of farm women provide dramatic confirmation of both findings. Farm women spend a great deal of time on housework. One study found that Alberta farm women spend as many as 66 hours per week, on average, doing housework.[31] Another national study of 200 farm families found that, on average, these women spent 42 hours a week on household work (and that those who were *not* employed off the farm did more housework — 43 hours — than those who were employed outside the home on a full-time basis — 36 hours.[32]

Studies also confirm that this work remains almost an exclusively female responsibility in farm families. One survey of 2,000 Quebec farm women indicated that 85% of the women were the only persons responsible for household work in their families.[33] A similar survey of 1,500 farm households in Alberta found that farm men contributed only about 10% of the total annual hours devoted to household work.[34] Finally, the national study found that farm husbands contributed between 6% and 12% of their time to household work, whereas women devoted about 85% of their time to it.[35]

These findings suggest that most farm households in Canada today have a relatively rigid division of labour, at least with respect to what is traditionally considered women's work. Most household tasks must be performed with daily regularity (for example, making of meals, washing of dishes, caring for children). On Canadian farms, as in Canadian cities, these tasks are performed by women, generally without assistance.

But the findings show that many farm women are involved *as well* in what is considered men's work: working in fields and barns, and doing farm maintenance and management. Furthermore, many farm women *also* hold paid jobs off the farm, creating the possibility of a triple workload. For most women, therefore, agricultural or off-farm work is *in addition* to the 40 hours per week they spend on household tasks — a heavy burden indeed!

Direct Assistance (Women's Work off the Farm)

As suggested in the previous sections, census figures and Labour Force Survey estimates indicate that women's direct involvement in agricultural work has increased between 1951 and 1983. Nevertheless, approximately one-third of female operators and spouses were employed mainly in non-agricultural occupations.

Why do farm women work off the farm? Given the economic situation of many family farms — a situation of high input costs and decreasing commodity prices — farm income must frequently be supplemented by off-farm income. Without off-farm income, some farms could not survive. Therefore, the majority of farm women who hold off-farm jobs do so out of economic necessity. One national study found that over half of employed farm women work to provide household necessities, to contribute to the farm operation, or to improve or maintain the family's standard of living; 35% of the women who worked off-farm reported investing over three-quarters of their personal incomes in the farm.[36] A study in Quebec revealed that 42% of farm women invested their incomes in the farm enterprise; most of that income was earned through off-farm work.[37]

Many families, therefore, rely on off-farm work to generate income to assist the farm operation. The following discussion examines changes and trends in the work of women off the farm, and analyses the extent of their direct assistance to agriculture.

■ Trends Between 1971 and 1981

More than one-quarter of women operators worked outside agriculture in 1981. This was more than double the percentage of women operators who reported non-agricultural occupations and hours in 1971. These women were also working more hours per week and more weeks per year at their non-agricultural jobs. Although less pronounced, the trend is similar for the many more women who were wives of operators and who reported non-agricultural hours, where the weeks per year have increased but the hours per week have dropped from 33 in 1971 to 32 in 1981.

Table 12: Average weekly hours and weeks per year, of women on farms in economic families with only one operator (or in a multi-operator family) and women with non-agricultural employment, Canada, 1971 and 1981.

	1971		1981	
	Operators	**Spouses**	**Operators**	**Spouses**
all women on farms	14,190	304,080	8,085	260,510
women with non-agricultural hours*	1,770	57,360	2,260	67,945
as a percentage of all women	12.5	18.9	27.9	26.1
average hours per week**	34	33	38	32
average weeks per year	35	34	36	35

Source: Canada, Statistics Canada, unpublished tabulations from the Agricultural Population Linkage, 1971 and 1981 Censuses.

Notes: Family farms include individual proprietorships, partnerships, and family corporations and excludes institutional, Hutterite, non-family corporations, and *other* farms and community pastures.

Economic families include two or more individuals living in the same dwelling, related to the census farm operator by birth, marriage, or adoption.
In 1981, families with more than one operator are excluded; in 1971, these were included.

   * Women without hours of work reported are excluded.
   ** In 1981, these are expressed as *hours last week*; they are "usual hours."

Relatively few female operators (12%) reported non-agricultural occupations in 1971. This figure increased to 28% in 1981. Women operators worked an average of 34 hours per week in non-agricultural occupations in 1971, and 38 hours in 1981. They also worked, on average, one week more per year (35 weeks in 1971, and 36 weeks in 1981).

Although the number of female spouses decreased by 14% between 1971 and 1981, the number of these women with non-agricultural occupations increased by 18%: from 57,360 to 67,945. These women also worked one week more per year, but one hour less per week.

Clearly, more women than ever on Canadian farms spend most of their work hours in non-agricultural occupations. Not only are there more women directly assisting family farms through off-farm work, but those who contribute in this way are doing so with greater intensity: they work more non-agricultural weeks per year than they did ten years ago.

■   Working both on and off the farm

Furthermore, many of these women *also* work directly on the farm. One study estimates that women who hold jobs off the farm also work at least 18 hours per week on the farm in tasks that contribute directly to agriculture.[38] Other research suggests that as many as 33% of operators and 17% of spouses with off-farm jobs work on the farm as well.[39] Because the census only counts a single main occupation, however, these hours do not ordinarily enter into estimates of women's direct contribution to agriculture. When these hours are taken into account, and added to previous estimates, it becomes apparent that women devote 2.5 million hours per week to agricultural work on the family farm.

In 1981, according to Table 11, female operators and spouses devoted 113,140 and 1,942,650 hours respectively to farm work. Table 13 adds these estimates to estimates of hours of unreported agricultural work done by female spouses and female operators who work mainly off the farm.

Women operators and spouses with off-farm occupations contributed at least another 283,374 hours to agriculture. By adding these hours to the hours spent by spouses and operators who work mainly on the farm, the total estimate for spouses and operators increases to 2,339,164, and the overall total of women's hours in direct agricultural work increases to 2,518,174 hours per week. This figure is probably a minimum estimate. It does not include the hours of on-farm work that may be contributed by other female family members who hold off-farm occupations, nor does it include the hours spent on household work, which, as mentioned above, may also include some direct agricultural work.

Table 13: Estimated additional hours directly involved in agriculture, by female operators and female spouses whose main occupation is non-agricultural

Types of Women	No. of Women Who Work Off the Farm	ESTIMATES		REVISED TOTALS			
		No. of Women Who Work Both Off and On the Farm*	Additional Hours**	Women***		Hours****	
				N	%	N	%
Operators	2,680	875	15,750	3,790	100	128,890	100
self-employed		760	13,680	3,280	87	114,545	89
paid		106	1,908	466	12	12,923	10
unpaid		9	162	44	1	1,422	1
Spouses	87,460	14,868	267,624	66,208	100	2,210,274	100
self-employed		5,501	99,018	24,251	37	867,863	39
paid		2,528	45,504	11,308	17	362,864	17
unpaid		6,839	123,102	30,649	46	979,547	44
Total	90,140	15,743	283,374	69,998	100	2,339,164	100
self-employed		6,261	112,698	27,531	39	982,408	42
paid		2,634	47,412	11,774	17	375,787	16
unpaid		6,848	123,264	30,693	44	980,969	42

Source: Frederick Buttel and Gilbert Gillespie, "Sexual Division of Farm Household Labour," *Rural Sociology*, vol. 49, no. 2 (1984); Susan Koski, *The Employment Practices of Farm Women* (Saskatoon: National Farmer's Union, 1982).

Notes: * These figures are estimated percentages of the number of women who work off the farm. Buttel and Gillespie estimate that 33% of men (operators) work off the farm and 17% of women (spouses) work off and on the farm. These figures have been added to the figures in the "number of women" column in Table 11.

** These additional hours are based on estimates of 18 hours of farm work per week done by women who work off the farm (see Koski, p. 29); these additional hours are calculated by multiplying the estimated number of women who work both off and on the farm by 18 hours per week.

*** These revised totals for the number of women are calculated in this table by adding the number of women who work off the farm to the number of "women with hours in agriculture" reported in Table 10.

**** These revised totals for the number of hours are calculated by adding the additional hours worked by women with off-farm occupations in this table to the "total weekly hours" reported in Table 11.

■ Women's off-farm occupations

A common assumption is that most farm women who work at jobs outside the farm are nurses or teachers in their local communities. In fact, the employment patterns for farm women with off-farm jobs differ little from those of other Canadian working women. Although one-quarter of operators and spouses do work in the fields of teaching and health, the majority (54%) are employed in the "pink-collar ghetto" of clerical, service, and sales occupations.

Figure 4 illustrates that there are some differences between women who are operators and those who are spouses.

Figure 4: Women on farms in mainly non-agricultural occupations, Canada, 1981

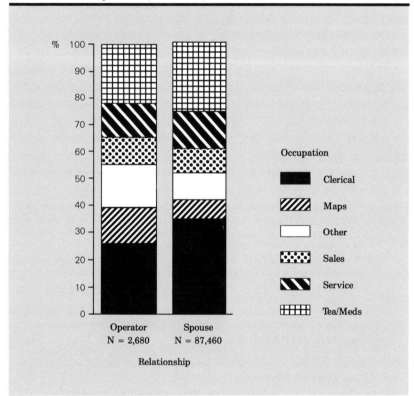

Source: Canada, Statistics Canada, unpublished tabulations from Agriculture Population Linkage, 1981 Censuses.

Note: *MAPS* includes managerial, administrative, and professional. *TEA/MEDS* includes teaching, medicine, and health.

For example, a greater percentage of spouses than operators worked in clerical occupations (35% compared to 26%); and operators (13%) were more likely than spouses (7%) to be employed in the managerial, administrative, and professional sectors. Nevertheless, 49% of all operators and 58% of all spouses who had non-agricultural jobs found them in the typically female clerical, sales, and service sectors, where approximately 57% of all other Canadian women find employment.[40]

The majority of women with off-farm jobs worked as paid employees. A small but notable percentage of the spouses, however, indicated that their work in non-agricultural occupations was unpaid. Spouses who are unpaid family workers appear in each of the occupational groups, but most are found in the clerical classification. This suggests the possibility that many of the 2,000 women who reported themselves as non-agriculturalists are, in fact, contributing directly to agriculture by keeping farm records. (See previous discussion of farm service and support tasks.)

In summary, these figures suggest that women on Canadian farms who work off the farm tend to be employed in occupations characterized by high rates of female participation.

WHAT INFLUENCES WOMEN'S WORK ON FAMILY FARMS?

Many factors influence the type and quantity of women's contributions to the family farm. Some of these are social factors; others are related to the type of farms on which women work. The following sections describe and examine some of these factors. The discussion of the relationship between women's contribution and farm type is based on national data sources. With respect to social factors, a national picture is not yet available. However, many regional studies have focussed on social factors — information is presented from these.

Social Factors Affecting Women's Contribution to the Family Farm

Although a national picture is not yet available, many regional studies have paid close attention to the social factors that have an impact on farm women. These studies have asked questions such as: What influences women's ability to make decisions regarding the farm? Are there significant regional differences that affect women's contribution? Is farm size related to women's involvement? Does the type of ownership have an influence? Does the level of women's capital contribution affect their participation? Do the number and ages of children alter women's work on, and contribution to, the farm? Only a few of the findings will be mentioned here, in part to illustrate the kinds of questions that social research in this area could address.

■ Regional differences

Although regional differences exist in women's contribution to the family farm, both national studies and national farm women's conferences suggest that the similarities are more striking than the differences. Farm women all over the country are united in identifying the financial crisis as the single most significant factor affecting their contribution to the family farm.[41] Regional differences exist to the extent that the economic stress is felt differently in each region. Thus, the specialization of commodity production by region emerges as an important variable affecting the types of women's participation. Some commodities are more sensitive to wide price variations than are others. Family farms in regions specializing in price-sensitive commodities tend to feel the farm-income crisis differently. This, in turn, may determine the way the women contribute to the farm. The greater the financial squeeze, the harder the whole family works and the greater the impact on the women who are, frequently, responsible for stress management within the family.

■ Decision making

Studies of husband-wife family farms show that men generally make most of the decisions related to the farm enterprise. Although farm husbands may consult their wives when borrowing money, purchasing land, or changing the commodity produced, the man usually retains the final say.[42] Some women are more involved than others in decision making; this level of involvement is thought to be influenced by a number of factors. In general, the greater the wife's active involvement in the enterprise, and the higher her awareness of farm issues, the greater her decision-making role. As well, the greater the number of children, the less involved the wife is in farm-enterprise decisions.[43] Women generally make decisions about their own work and about many daily farm tasks, but have less influence than their male partners on the direction of the farm operation.[44] Farm women have almost no voice in agriculture policy, or in the directions taken by farm organizations.[45]

■ Age

According to one Prince Edward Island study, women in the middle-age range are more involved than are older or younger women in barn and field work, and in management tasks; the older the woman, the more involved she is in supervisory work. Older women, however, are also less involved in decisions about commodities.[46] When age is considered a factor, it is also necessary to examine the stages of a woman's life cycle, and that of her family and the farm. For example, the less frequent involvement of younger women in field and barn work may be related to their child-rearing responsibilities: women in the middle-age range generally do not have as many pre-schoolers and babies to look after during the day, and therefore might be able to get outside more easily to work.

■ Children

The number and ages of children do have some small relationship to the type of work done by women on the farm,[47] and may have an even stronger bearing on the way women feel about that work. Women have reported that one of the greatest personal stresses they face is the degree to which farm work distracts them from attending to their children's needs: whether or not there are children, the farm work must be done at certain times of the day, and during certain seasons. There is little or no opportunity in today's farm family for alternative child care — few farm families can rely on grandparents or other relatives to care for the young ones while their mothers go out to the fields. Group child-care facilities are extremely rare in most farming communities. Consequently, many women who work directly on the farm are frequently forced to take young children with them, exposing them to the dangers inherent in working with heavy machinery, chemicals, etc.

The P.E.I. study also found that a higher percentage of women with young children (aged one to five) are engaged in off-farm employment than are women with older children.[48] This circumstance reflects the farm life cycle. A younger farm family — one that is just starting to become established — must purchase equipment and land to a greater extent than must an older farm family. Younger farm women are thus led to seek outside employment to generate the necessary income. The degree to which younger women differ in education or training from older women, giving them more readily marketable skills, may also be a factor. Younger women may be able to secure off-farm employment more easily.

With respect to the age-related differences in women's work mentioned above, it is worth noting that women's workload on the farm tends to change as their children grow up: older children often relieve their mothers of some of the direct farm work,[49] and also may be more involved in household work.

■ Farm size

Studies suggest that women tend to be less involved in direct farm work on larger farms. However, one study found that farm size itself is not the main factor; rather, the level of mechanization and specialization that occurs in larger farms results in work patterns different from patterns on mixed commodity farms with lower levels of mechanization.[50] In simple farming operations, women have broader involvement. They are more active in decision making, and also do a greater variety of jobs. More highly mechanized or specialized farms may entail a greater division of work. Men carry out more specialized farm tasks, while women perform the managerial work of bookkeeping, maintaining market information, and dealing with supplies and services.

■ Farm ownership
The structure of farm ownership seems to have some influence on the way women work on the farm. The P.E.I. study suggests that women are more involved in barn and field work, as well as in management tasks, where the husband and wife are formally in partnership.[51] The extent of women's financial investment in the farm also appears to be related to the type of work that women do on the farm. Women who make a capital contribution toward the purchase of land, buildings, and machinery, for example, tend to be more involved in farm animal care, repair and maintenance of machinery, and management.[52]

The Relationship Between Women's Contribution and Farm Type
There are several ways in which farms can be defined, and there are also different types of farms. Farms differ, for example, in the way in which they are legally organized and constituted. As well, farms specialize in producing different products. Finally, farms differ according to how much money they earn from sales. The literature on farm women indicates that their contribution may vary according to the type of farm on which they live. For example, it has been suggested that women from farms that produce a certain type of commodity will have off-farm jobs more frequently than will women on other types of farms.

The interactions between farm type and the nature and extent of women's contribution are complex. The following section restricts itself to asking three questions about the way in which farm type and women's contribution may be related. Are women who contribute economically to the family farm through income earned off the farm more likely than are other farm women to be considered business partners in the farm enterprise? Is the work of women from farms that produce certain commodities different from that of women in other areas of commodity production? Is women's contribution to direct agricultural work primarily made on hobby or marginal farms rather than on larger commercial farms?

■   Type of legal organization

There are four basic types of organization for family farms in Canada: individual or family farms; partnership farms with a written agreement; partnership farms without a written agreement; and "a legally constituted company in which the shares are owned mostly by him and his family or with most of the shares owned by other person(s) or business."[53]

Most Canadian farms are run by individuals or families, although this percentage is decreasing. In 1971, 92% of all Canadian farms were individual or family farms; by 1981, only 87% were classified in this way.[54] The percentage of partnership farms (both written and unwritten partnerships) increased during the same period, from 6% in 1971 to 10% in 1981. Very few farms were classified as family corporations in either 1971 (2%) or 1981 (3%).

Unfortunately, national data sources do not specify the sex of legal partners or shareholders. It is therefore impossible to estimate how many of the partners on family farms are women, or how many women are shareholders in farm corporations.

However, as shown in Table 14, there is a slight tendency for farms that are *not* characterized by off-farm work to be either written partnerships or family corporations. It does not appear, therefore, that women who contribute economically to the family farm through off-farm employment are any more likely than would those who work on the farm to be partners or shareholders in these farms. (The implications of this finding can be best assessed in light of the discussion regarding legal rights of farm women in Michelle Boivin's article.) The predominance in Canada, however, of single-owner or family farms underscores the acute necessity for spouses of operators to have their work formally recognized.

■   Type of commodities

Canadian family farms tend to specialize in a single type of production. Table 15 shows that one in three farms produces wheat or small grains, almost one-quarter of the farms raise cattle, and almost 15% are dairy farms. Less than 6% (16,155) are mixed farms.

The type of commodity may affect the economic well-being of the family farm. Relatively low levels of gross sales or relatively low income from certain commodities may, in turn, affect the amount of work done off and on the farm. Certainly, the type of commodity itself may also dictate the amount of both types of work.

Trying to measure women's contribution to Canadian agriculture

Table 14: Off-farm work typology for male operators and female spouses on family farms, by type of organization, Canada, 1981

Type of Organization	NO OFF-FARM WORK		OPERATOR ONLY		SPOUSE ONLY		BOTH OFF-FARM		TOTAL		
	N	% row	N	% row	N	% row	N	% row	N	% row	% col.
Individual Proprietorship	131,540	54.5	40,060	16.6	37,275	15.5	32,365	13.4	241,240	100	86.7
Partnership:											
no written agreement	9,775	59.6	1,850	11.3	2,675	16.3	2,100	12.8	16,400	100	5.9
with written agreement	7,065	63.8	1,100	9.9	1,760	15.9	1,155	10.4	11,080	100	4.0
Family Corporation	5,995	63.4	970	10.2	1,485	15.7	1,010	10.7	9,460	100	3.4
Total	154,375	55.5	43,980	15.8	43,195	15.5	36,630	13.2	278,180	100	100

Source: Canada, Statistics Canada, unpublished tabulations from Agriculture Population Linkage, 1981 Censuses.

Table 15: Off-farm work typology for male operators and female spouses on family farms with only one operator, by type of farm, Canada, 1981

Type of Farm	Total Number of Farms	No Off-Farm Work	OFF-FARM WORK			Total	
			Operator Only	Spouse Only	Both		
		%	%	%	%	row	% col.
Dairy	41,420	79.5	5.4	12.8	2.3	100	14.9
Cattle	64,390	47.7	21.2	15.1	16.0	100	23.2
Hogs	12,435	55.9	15.4	17.1	11.6	100	4.5
Poultry	7,830	42.5	26.1	10.9	20.5	100	2.8
Wheat/Small Grains	95,700	56.7	12.2	18.9	12.2	100	34.4
Other Field Crops	10,970	52.2	19.1	11.3	17.4	100	3.9
Fruit and Vegetable	12,960	46.7	22.3	11.6	19.3	100	4.7
Misc. Specialty	16,325	36.3	27.4	12.3	24.0	100	5.9
Mixed Farms	16,155	51.8	18.7	14.8	14.7	100	5.8
Total	278,185	55.5	15.8	15.5	13.2	100	100

Source: Canada, Statistics Canada, unpublished tabulations from Agriculture Population Linkage, 1981 Censuses.

Dairy production, for example, is relatively labour-intensive. Wheat farming is machinery- and land-intensive, whereas other types of commodities do not rely on both machinery and land to such a degree. Still other commodities, such as cattle, require large investments in land and relatively smaller investments in machinery.

It is therefore reasonable to expect that the type of commodity will have some relationship to the type of work that farm women and men do on and off the farm. Census data confirm this expectation.

Off-farm work
The type of commodity produced does affect the tendency of farm

husbands and/or wives to work off the farm. The most striking example is the difference between dairy farms and other types of commodities. For example, Table 15 shows that in over three-quarters of dairy farms, neither the operator nor the spouse worked off the farm, whereas only 36% of miscellaneous specialty farms reported no off-farm work by operators or spouses. What might explain these differences? Dairy farming is supply-managed and subsidized; might these be factors alleviating the need to supplement farm income through off-farm employment? Furthermore, do the number of hours involved in dairy farming make it more difficult to undertake work off the farm? Reasons for these differences in the prevalence of off-farm work merit further investigation.

The complex interaction between husbands' and wives' on-farm and off-farm work patterns, suggested by other studies,[55] is also confirmed by the figures reported in Table 15. Dairy farms are least likely to have either the operator (5%) or the operator and spouse (2%) working off the farm. In this type of farm, if anyone works off the farm, it tends to be the spouse alone (13%). In contrast, farms with relatively high rates of off-farm work (miscellaneous specialty, poultry, fruit and vegetable, and cattle farms) are those in which either the operator or both operator and spouse are most likely to work off the farm. Finally, wheat/small grain and hog farms are the most likely (19% and 17% respectively, compared to 15% for the total) to report *spouse only* off-farm work.

One U.S. study, based on an examination of work patterns on dairy farms, suggested that there is "a tendency for farm men and women to specialize mutually in either on-farm or off-farm work."[56] The Canadian figures presented on Table 15 suggest that this conclusion may not hold true for all types of farms.

In addition, the amount of work that women operators do off the farm varies according to the type of farm they operate (although farm type is not related to spouses' off-farm hours). Generally, female operators of miscellaneous specialty farms work a greater proportion of hours in non-agricultural jobs than do those who operate poultry, small grain, and other field-crop farms.[57]

On-farm work

What is the relationship between the type of commodity, the number of female operators and spouses who are active in agriculture, and the number of hours they report having worked on the farm? Women operators are concentrated in certain types of commodity production, and underrepresented in others, as can be seen in Table 16.

Once again, dairy farming seems to be exceptional. In 1981, almost 15% of all economic family farms in Canada were dairy farms and 15% of female operators ran dairy farms in that year. Other commodities, however, show both extremes. For example, female operators are responsible for 18% of miscellaneous specialty farms, but these represent under 6% of all farms. Women also operate almost 9% of fruit and vegetable farms, which represent less than 5% of all family farms. In contrast, women rarely operate wheat or small grain farms (under 9% in each category) although one out of three Canadian family farms is in wheat/small grains production.

Table 16 also reveals a different pattern for *wives* of operators. For example, almost 25% of all spouses worked on dairy farms, although these were, as noted above, only 15% of all farms. Less than 18% of wives worked on cattle farms, which represent 23% of Canadian farms. The situation on wheat and small grain farms is similar: 29% of wives worked on these farms, which account for 34% of all Canadian farms.

When the hours that women devote to direct agricultural work are taken into consideration, the pattern becomes even more complex. For example, wives of dairy farm operators represented nearly 25% of all spouses working directly in agriculture, but they worked almost one-third (29%) of all spouses' hours. An opposite trend occurs with spouses of wheat and small grain operators. These women represent 14% and 15% of all spouses whose main occupation was agricultural; yet only 11% and 13% of all spouses' hours were worked on wheat and small grain farms respectively. Other than these, there are no noteworthy differences.

The findings suggest that commodity type does influence whether women work, and the amount of work they do on farms. Specifically, wives of dairy farm operators work a greater proportion of the hours contributed by spouses directly involved in agriculture, whereas spouses of wheat and small grain farm operators contribute fewer hours on an annual basis. It would be useful to investigate which factors contribute to the difference in the amount of work done by spouses on the two types of farms.

Table 16: Women's agricultural hours on family farms, by type of farm, Canada, 1981

	NUMBER AND % OF FARMS		WOMEN WITH AGRICULTURAL HOURS							
			Female Operators				Female Spouses			
			PERSONS		Annual Hours (000s)		PERSONS		Annual Hours (000s)	
	N	%	N	%	N	%	N	%	N	%
Dairy	41,420	14.9	450	15.4	1,053	18.3	12,610	24.6	24,150	28.8
Cattle	64,390	23.1	675	23.2	1,266	22.0	9,015	17.6	14,717	17.5
Hogs	12,435	4.5	125	4.3	285	5.0	2,745	5.3	4,122	4.9
Poultry	7,830	2.8	120	4.1	224	3.9	1,460	2.8	2,108	2.5
Wheat	46,330	16.7	205	7.0	350	6.1	7,000	13.6	9,297	11.1
Small Grains	49,370	17.7	245	8.4	542	9.4	7,810	15.2	11,209	13.4
Other Field	10,970	3.9	115	3.9	230	4.0	2,280	4.4	3,951	4.7
Fruit/Vegetable	12,960	4.7	250	8.6	369	6.4	2,665	5.2	3,678	4.4
Misc. Specialty	16,325	5.9	530	18.2	1,048	18.2	2,495	4.9	4,646	5.5
Mixed Livestock	9,710	3.4	125	4.3	289	5.0	2,310	4.5	4,336	5.2
Mixed Field Crop	535	0.2	5	0.2	21	0.4	155	0.3	256	0.3
Mixed Other	5,910	2.1	70	2.4	74	1.3	810	1.6	1,422	1.7
Total	278,185	100	2,915	100	5,751	100	51,355	100	83,892	100

Source: Canada, Statistics Canada, unpublished tabulations from Agriculture Population Linkage, 1981 Censuses.

■ Level of gross sales

As mentioned above, farms also vary according to how much the farm families earn from what they sell. *Gross sales* refers to the dollars received by farm families for agricultural products, before deducting operating expenses, such as fuel, fertilizer, interest, and labour payments. In 1981, purchased inputs (a concept that may underrepresent the cost of all operating expenses) constituted 66% of the value of production on all Canadian farms.[58] Family farms with gross sales of at least $21,805 were considered commercial operations in 1981. Half of all Canadian farms were commercial farms; these produced 93% of the total commodities marketed in 1981.[59] Certain types of farms (dairy, cattle, wheat, and small grain) are more likely to be classified as commercial farms. Other commodity types (such as poultry, miscellaneous specialty, and fruit and vegetable) tend to have, on average, lower gross sales.

It has been suggested that women are less involved on those farms classified as *commercial*, and more involved in farms with relatively low gross sales (marginal or hobby farms). The following analysis examines whether women's hours of agricultural work are, in fact, disproportionately devoted to types of farms with relatively low gross sales, that is, whether women work on real farms. This analysis is done by comparing the hours of female and male operators and those of spouses on all farms and on commercial farms.

Table 17 indicates that there are remarkably different answers to the question: "Do women work on real farms?" These answers seem to depend, in part, on whether the women are spouses of operators or are operators themselves.

For example, 18% of all female operators' agricultural hours were worked on dairy farms, but these comprised 30% of all hours worked by women on commercial dairy farms. This suggests that, contrary to the expectations of some researchers, female operators of dairy farms are more likely to work on those operations with relatively *higher* gross sales. The same trend holds for female operators of hog and wheat farms, although there are few female operators of wheat commodity farms. On the other hand, there is also a large number of female operators who work in commodities with lower gross sales, particularly miscellaneous specialty, but also poultry and mixed livestock farms.

Women operators had an average total income from all sources in 1981 of $10,787 — almost $7,000 less than that of male operators.[60] This may be due in part to the disproportionate number of women who operate farms with relatively low gross sales, such as miscellaneous specialty farms, and the small number of women running wheat or small grain farms, which tend to have higher gross sales.

As well, the findings illustrated in Table 17 suggest that the average income figure may mask the existence of two distinct groups of female operators with different levels of income: those who worked a considera-

Table 17: Percentage distribution of all operators' and spouses' annual agricultural hours on family farms with only one operator in an economic family, and on farms with sales of $21,805+, Canada, 1981

| | OPERATORS | | | | SPOUSES | | | |
| | MALE | | FEMALE | | MALE | | FEMALE | |
	All %	With Sales $21,805+ %	All %	With Sales $21,805+ %	All %	With Sales $21,805+ %	All %	With Sales $21,805+ %
Dairy	23.4	26.3	18.3	29.9	19.6	26.8	28.8	32.6
Cattle	19.1	15.5	22.0	16.7	15.9	12.1	17.5	14.7
Hogs	5.0	5.4	4.9	7.9	4.6	6.2	4.9	5.4
Poultry	1.7	1.8	3.9	2.3	1.9	—	2.5	2.6
Wheat	17.9	18.9	6.1	7.9	12.1	11.5	11.1	11.6
Small Grains	19.3	19.9	9.4	9.5	16.2	21.1	13.4	14.0
Other Field	2.6	2.8	4.0	5.1	2.1	2.5	4.7	5.6
Fruit/Vegetable	2.8	2.2	6.4	5.0	6.8	4.2	4.4	3.5
Misc. Specialty	2.8	1.8	18.2	11.8	14.9	13.4	5.5	3.8
Mixed Livestock	3.9	3.7	5.0	2.5	2.6	—	5.2	4.4
Mixed Field Crop	0.2	0.3	0.4	—	—	—	0.3	0.4
Mixed Other	1.4	1.3	1.3	1.3	3.2	2.0	1.7	1.4
Total	100	100	100	100	100	100	100	100

Source: Canada, Statistics Canada, unpublished tabulations from Agriculture Population Linkage, 1981 Censuses.

ble number of hours on farms with relatively high levels of gross sales, such as dairy farms; and another sizeable group involved in farms with low gross sales, such as cattle and miscellaneous specialty farms.

Contrary to popular opinion, spouses did not, in fact, contribute a disproportionate number of hours to those farms with low gross sales. For example, although dairy farms represent 23% of all farms operated by men, and 26% of all commercial farms, female spouses were directly involved in agricultural work on 29% of all dairy farms, and on 33% of dairy farms with at least average gross sales. Furthermore, although wives' hours were underrepresented on wheat, small grain, and poultry farms, these hours were worked on commercial farms. The only exceptions to this trend were cattle, mixed livestock, and miscellaneous specialty farms.

Therefore, although the distribution of annual hours contributed by spouses and operators to various commodity and sales levels suggests some diversity, this analysis shows that women's work is not disproportionately devoted to farms with low gross sales. Contrary to a commonly held assumption, women work directly in agriculture on commercial farms and not only, or primarily, on farms with marginal gross sales.

WOMEN IN AGRICULTURAL EDUCATION AND
FARM ORGANIZATIONS

177

**Trying to
measure
women's
contribution
to Canadian
agriculture**

The gender composition of Canadian agriculture is changing — or at
least, women's participation is becoming more evident. As discussed
earlier, women have become much more involved in primary agriculture
over the past 30 years. They are also becoming more involved in
secondary agricultural occupations, working in greater numbers as
agricultural representatives and researchers, dairy scientists, livestock
field agents, and other occupations. In 1961, for example, a mere 2% of
agriculturalists and related scientists were female; by 1981, women
represented 12% of this group.[61]

Is this greater involvement reflected in other aspects of agricultural
life? Are farm women, as a consequence of their increased visibility in
agricultural production, becoming more involved in organizations that
represent or provide services to Canadian farm families? Are women
becoming more involved in agricultural programs at Canadian universities and colleges? The following discussion addresses these questions and
briefly reviews some of the work being done by farm women themselves to
ensure that their essential contribution is recognized.

Women's Participation In Agricultural Education

Canada's first female judge of Holsteins, Joan McNeely, remembers looking
. . . out the classroom window in home economics back in the 50s, envying
the young men studying animal husbandry. 'A young woman didn't study
agriculture in those days. But I wish I had.'[62]

With a few exceptions,[63] most of the literature on trends in agricultural
education or employment is bereft of any mention of women's involvement. Some recent studies[64] no longer mistakenly assume that agriculture is a male occupation,[65] but fail to analyse the trends reported in
terms of either gender. Public policy in Canada is not, and never has been,
gender-neutral. Not discriminating against women does not imply that
gender — as a factor — ought to be ignored entirely.[66] From this
perspective, analyses of trends in the agricultural labour force and in

education programs remain incomplete if both men's and women's involvement are not recognized.

■ Enrolment and graduation rates

More and more Canadian women are acquiring a university education. In the past 15 years, women's participation in Canadian universities has greatly increased. For example, between 1972 and 1981, the total number of women enrolled in university programs jumped by 54%, while that of men rose by only 7%.[67] This trend is even more remarkable in the agricultural sciences, as shown in Table 18.

Table 18: Enrolments at faculties of agriculture, by type of enrolment and sex,* in Canadian universities, 1975-76 and 1984-85

	NUMBER	% OF TOTAL	% CHANGE (1975 = 100)
1975-76: Total Students	5,380	100	
male	4,068	75.6	
female	1,312	24.4	
Full-Time	5,124	95.2	
male	3,865	71.8	
female	1,259	23.4	
Part-Time	256	4.8	
male	203	3.8	
female	53	1.0	
1984-85: Total Students	6,494	100	20.7
male	4,120	63.4	1.3
female	2,374	36.6	80.9
Full-Time	5,980	92.1	16.7
male	3,806	58.6	-1.5
female	2,174	33.5	72.7
Part-Time	514	7.9	100.8
male	314	4.8	54.7
female	200	3.1	277.4

Sources: Canada, Statistics Canada, unpublished special tabulations, University Student Information System. See also: *Universities: enrolment and degrees* (catalogue no. 81-204).

Note: * Excludes interns and residents.

Between 1972 and 1981, the total number of women enrolled in agriculture programs in Canadian universities jumped from 1,312 to 2,374 — an increase of 81% — while the number of men increased by under 2%. These gains are reflected in the figures in Table 18: in 1975, under one-quarter of agriculture students were female; ten years later, this figure had climbed to 37%.

Not only are more women than ever before enrolling in agriculture programs, but more of them are graduating.

Table 19 shows that 20% of all graduates were female in 1975; by 1985, 39% were female. In fact, female students were more likely to complete the degree programs than were male students.

Other studies of educational participation have found that women were less likely to complete graduate degrees than were men, and that they were more likely to enrol in traditionally female programs. These trends have been apparent in faculties of agriculture in the past. To illustrate, although women represented 20% of all 1975 agriculture graduates, less than 9% were in plant science. In the same year, the overwhelming majority (94%) of master's degrees in animal science were granted to men. Not a single woman obtained a doctorate in animal science from a Canadian faculty of agriculture in 1975 (Table 19).

This trend has been changing in recent years, however. Only 28% of all master's degree enrolments in Canadian universities were female in 1971; by 1981, that figure had reached 41%.[68] In addition, recent studies reveal that women are entering a wider range of programs than ever before. Representation of women in agriculture science, a traditionally male field, doubled between 1972 and 1982.[69]

Within agriculture programs, similar changes have occurred. In 1975, for example, only 13% of master's degrees and 10% of doctoral degrees were granted to women; the figures more than doubled by 1984, when women obtained more than 34% of master's degrees and almost 22% of doctoral degrees at faculties of agriculture (Table 19). Women agriculture students are also much more likely to be involved in traditionally male specializations today than they were ten years ago. For example, women are now graduating from plant science and animal science programs at a rate almost equal to, or greater than, the average rate of graduation.

Despite these encouraging advances, it should be noted that male students continue to be more likely than do females to complete

Table 19: Graduates of faculties of agriculture, by type of degree, field of study, and sex, in Canadian universities, 1975 and 1984

	Animal Science	% Row	% col	Plant Science	% Row	% Col	Soil Science	% Row	% Col	Other	% Row	% Col	Total	% Row	% Col
1975: Total graduates	143	21.3	100	123	18.3	100	31	4.6	100	375	55.8	100	672	100	100
– male	119		83.2	112		91.1	23		74.2	284		75.7	538		80.1
– female	24		16.8	11		8.9	8		25.8	91		24.3	134		19.9
Bachelors	116	21.8	100	73	13.7	100	17	3.2	100	327	61.3	100	533	100	100
– male	93		80.2	65		89.0	12		70.6	246		75.2	416		78.0
– female	23		19.8	8		11.0	5		29.4	81		24.8	117		22.0
Masters	18	18.0	100	35	35.0	100	11	11.0	100	36	36.0	100	100	100	100
– male	17		94.4	32		91.4	9		81.8	29		80.6	87		87.0
– female	1		5.6	3		8.6	2		18.2	7		19.4	13		13.0
Doctorate	9	23.1	100	15	38.5	100	3	7.7	100	12	30.8	100	39	100	100
– male	9		100	15		100	2		66.7	9		75.0	35		89.7
– female	–		–	–		–	1		33.3	3		25.0	4		10.3
1984: Total graduates	125	15.7	100	280	35.1	100	66	8.3	100	327	41.0	100	798	100	100
– male	74		59.2	174		62.1	54		81.8	183		56.0	485		60.8
– female	51		40.8	106		37.9	12		18.2	144		44.0	313		39.2
Bachelors	69	13.0	100	173	32.6	100	24	4.5	100	265	49.9	100	531	100	100
– male	36		52.2	102		59.0	18		75.0	147		55.5	303		57.1
– female	33		47.8	71		41.0	6		25.0	118		44.5	228		42.9
Masters	46	21.7	100	83	39.2	100	34	16.0	100	49	23.1	100	212	100	100
– male	31		67.4	53		63.9	28		82.4	27		55.1	139		65.6
– female	15		32.6	30		36.1	6		17.6	22		44.9	73		34.4
Doctorate	10	18.2	100	24	43.6	100	8	14.6	100	13	23.6	100	55	100	100
– male	7		70.0	19		79.2	8		100	9		69.2	43		78.2
– female	3		30.0	5		20.8	–		–	4		30.8	12		21.8

Source: Canada, Statistics Canada. Unpublished special tabulations, University Student Information System. See also: *Universities...: enrolment and degrees* (catalogue no. 81-204).

doctorates in agriculture as well as in other fields of university study. Advances into male fields of specialization are uneven as well: fewer women graduated from soil science programs in 1984 than in 1975.

■ Women's increased participation and its impact on colleges or faculties of agriculture

A telephone survey of 13 Canadian administrators showed that most colleges or faculties of agriculture (80%) had experienced increases in women's enrolment during the last decade. How have colleges or faculties of agriculture responded to women's greater involvement in agricultural education?

According to the administrators, most colleges or faculties have not changed their programs. However, reasons for the lack of change vary.

Some administrators appear to believe that special measures are not required. For them, leaving the curriculum unchanged reflects their view that women and men are treated equally within their programs. This is illustrated by one administrator's response:

> Women on our faculty — 10 out of 60 teachers — say that too much fuss is being made of this (the increase). It is not a new phenomenon. We are also hiring more women faculty, though we're not actively recruiting more female professors or students — it's just occurring naturally.

Although they report no program changes, other college or faculty administrators have a more positive view. They speak highly of their female students' accomplishments and enthusiastically about their effect on the courses and student life. For them, women's greater involvement is a welcome development.

> We always knew that women could do what men can do. The problem was in stereotyped views out there on the farm — and it still is, to some extent. It's still a man's world on the farm; that's how the public perceives it, too. At our college, women can do all the things that men can do. We know it and we encourage them.

Faculties of agriculture that *have* responded to women's growing participation are in the decided minority (8%). Only one university administrator reported modifications. Changes that he reported "to address the interests of women in primary agriculture" include: establishment of a faculty and student standing committee to investigate and report on women's issues; increased recognition in curricula of women as illustrations and examples of work in agricultural production;

and similar adjustments to program content. These changes in the agriculture faculty are part of a more general effort within the university to recruit more women students.

Most administrators (62%) felt that women graduates were as successful as were male graduates in finding employment after graduation. A significant minority (38%), however, felt that women experienced greater difficulty, and *none* suggested that female students might have greater chances of success in finding employment than might male students.

Those who felt that women had chances equal with those of men implied that this was a relatively recent phenomenon, and attributed it to changing attitudes on the part of employers: "Employers are changing their attitudes as their experiences in hiring women turn out to be quite positive — more doors are opening for women"; or: "Employers are increasingly gender-blind — they just want the top students."

Others were less optimistic about women's opportunities. For example, one commented that, although women are now finding jobs in animal and plant science and in agricultural economics, male graduates are still more successful in finding employment in other areas. These administrators attributed women's difficulties in finding employment to employers' attitudes, especially in private industry. They also held out some hope that these attitudes were changing, although at different rates in different locations. For example, one university administrator commented: "Large companies don't seem to discriminate. Smaller companies and family businesses discriminate only until they've hired a female or have made close observation of another firm employing a woman."

Sex-stereotyped practices and attitudes *on the farm* were also mentioned as limiting women's potential employment opportunities. One administrator described the progress of one female student as follows: "She wanted to be in our Production and Management program — our on-farm program — but her father refused. So she went into the Business and Commerce stream at our college and now works for the provincial Ministry."

In summary, although women's participation in all fields of agricultural study continues to increase dramatically, this has not resulted in modifications to the programs in most faculties of agriculture. Very little attention has been paid to women's increased involvement in agricultural production or education. Nor have programs been developed to serve their specific needs. Although women are graduating in higher numbers than ever before, they may face discrimination in the job market. Most administrators feel that employer attitudes, perceptions of the general public, and sex-stereotyped practices on the farm affect women's employment opportunities; however, they also feel that attitudes are changing in a positive direction.

It should be noted that women involved in agricultural work have long been concerned about the lack of available training programs. They need specialized programs to further enhance women's ability to contribute to the operation of family farms. Some training programs with an adult education focus are being experimented with to meet these needs.

Women's Participation in Agricultural Organizations

Agricultural organizations play an essential role in Canadian farming, and form an integral part of rural life. There are approximately 450 organizations representing or serving Canadian farm families. Some represent specific commodities or producers; some are concerned with marketing; others offer services to farm families; still others represent their general interests.

Farm women have expressed serious concern about women's lack of involvement in farm organizations, and their lack of representation in leadership positions within these organizations. The literature generally confirms this perception, and various studies suggest different reasons for this inequality. Some authors link women's lack of participation to impediments in the structure or practices of farm organizations themselves. For example, some point out that only husbands in farm families are assumed to have voting rights in farm organizations;[70] others suggest that women's involvement is encouraged only up to certain levels.[71] Some farm organizations are reportedly unsympathetic to women's involvement, are reluctant to address women's issues, and make few real efforts to overcome barriers to women's participation (for example, providing child care to facilitate women's attendance at meetings).[72]

Other authors suggest that women themselves, to some extent, are responsible for their lack of involvement in farm organizations. For example, many women are not certain if they have a contribution to make, do not know how to make it, and tend to regard themselves as responsible solely for domestic activities, thereby limiting their own opportunities.[73] This perspective finds impediments to women's participation within women themselves, or within farm families, rather than within organizations.

Yet others attempt to understand farm women's lack of access in terms of their position in the economic and political process. One Saskatchewan group suggests that the division of labour in farm organizations clearly reflects women's limited access to economic and political power in general, and is reinforced by a tradition of male dominance:

> We live in a society which measures worth in terms of dollars, thus, despite the double and sometimes triple workload (farm, household and wage labour), women feel and are made to feel that their labour is not really 'work' — at least not the sort of work which entitles them to an equal role in the decision making process.[74]

Canadian farm women are recognizing that they need to become actively involved in farm organizations in order to represent their own special interests as women, but also to add their perspectives and abilities to efforts to improve the policies and practices that affect all farm families. Women on farms have served as sandwich-makers and banquet-servers for meetings in which they could not participate.[75] They "are no longer willing to be relegated to an upstairs room or basement to watch a cooking demonstration or fashion show", while the men make policy decisions,[76] and they want more than token representation on organizations that serve farm families.

To develop *effective* strategies for increasing women's participation in farm organizations, however, it is first necessary to identify the *specific* barriers that keep women out. In an attempt to pinpoint some of these barriers, this section analyses the results of a survey of selected farm organizations. (Appendix C provides a more detailed methodology, and a list of organizations approached is given in Appendix D.) This survey is only a first step in systematically examining the barriers that keep women out of farm organizations, and inevitably raises more questions than it answers. Nevertheless, it is hoped the results will encourage further investigation and stimulate discussion on methods to facilitate women's involvement.

Awareness of women in agriculture
The majority of farm organizations (75%) felt that women have become more involved in primary Canadian agriculture in the last decade. Most attributed this to the increasing complexity of farms; others to a change in women's own attitudes, or changes in women's training and skills; several pointed to changes in attitudes towards women. Many mentioned the increasing economic pressures experienced by farm families, which result in wives substituting for hired labour.

Membership
Despite the above-mentioned awareness, women are in fact underrepresented in farm organizations. Over a third (35%) of the organizations surveyed did not know what percentage of their members were women. Only half of those that could provide an estimate had more than 30% female members. One-quarter estimated women to represent 10% to 29% of their members. A mere 5% of the organizations offered separate membership for operator and spouse.

Leadership
Leadership of farm organizations was almost exclusively male. Most (86%) of the organizations had an elected governing body, usually composed of no more than 20 persons. In over half of the organizations (54%), no women held elected positions. In one out of three organizations, women represented less than a third of the elected leadership. Only 12% of the organizations had women in at least 30% of their senior policy positions.

Recruitment of women
Most organizations have made no effort to recruit women. Very few (13%) have made provisions to ensure women's representation in elected positions, or to increase the number of women members (17%). Approximately one-third of the organizations have created programs directed toward women in agriculture, or have aimed to increase women's organizational involvement.

Obstacles to women's participation
Only one in four organizations recognized that obstacles existed within

their own organizations. Two-thirds of these felt that people's attitudes were the problem. (The attitudes of men and women were blamed in equal degree.) Fifty-six per cent of all the organizations surveyed had some requirements for membership, such as a production minimum, a licence or quota to produce, or grower registration. The great majority (90%), however, did not believe that these requirements inhibited the participation of women in their organizations. Twenty per cent felt the main inhibiting factor was that women tend not to be "designated producers". One respondent stated that "women tend to have to stay at home while their husbands are off making policy."

■ Differences among types of organizations

Some types of organizations were more able than others to estimate the sex of their membership. For example, organizations that "serve farm families" (such as marketing boards, retail co-operatives, credit unions, or federations of agriculture) were less able to estimate the percentage of women members than were those organizations representing commodity or other interests of farm families.

But knowledge does not necessarily translate into action. Among the very organizations that knew how many members were female, commodity interest groups were least likely to have women on their governing bodies. On the other hand, those representing general interests of farm families were most likely to have women in 30% or more of the elected positions.

At the same time, lack of knowledge is not related to inaction. As an illustration, federations of agriculture were among those organizations least able to estimate the percentage of their female membership. Nevertheless, 43% of the federations had women in 10% to 20% of their elected positions.

Commodity associations and marketing boards or agencies have made little effort to increase female membership. These organizations were least likely to have developed programs directed toward women in agriculture, and more likely to feel that organizational impediments to women's involvement do not exist.

National organizations differed considerably from regional/provincial bodies. Although few of the national organizations were able to provide information on female membership, 36% had elected women to at least one out of three leadership positions, in marked contrast to the 4%

of provincial associations with at least 30% women leaders. While national organizations were no more likely than were provincial ones to have developed programs directed toward women, or to recognize organizational impediments to women's involvement, they were more likely to have made efforts to increase women's participation.

There were some differences among organizations based in different provinces. Those from Quebec, Ontario, and British Columbia were least likely to have women in leadership positions. Quebec and Ontario organizations were also more likely to report having no female members. The practices of the provincial organizations, however, did not vary a great deal. Only those based in the Maritime provinces had made above-average efforts to increase women's membership. Reasons for the special concern to involve women in the Maritimes merit further investigation.

In summary, most organizations representing or serving Canadian farm families are aware that women's involvement in primary agriculture is increasing. This increase, however, is not reflected in their memberships, and even less in the leadership of the great majority of these organizations.

The results of this survey confirm what has been already well documented. Most farm organizations do not appear to be interested in encouraging women to examine the factors preventing them from participating, or to help circumvent these stumbling-blocks. Although individual respondents appeared sensitive to, and concerned about, women's lack of involvement, these results suggest that the status quo has changed very little since 1981.

> The onus is always on the individual, not on an analysis of why women are not presently in leadership roles, why they lack the necessary skills or confidence, nor on the role that men must play in freeing women for active involvement. None of the organizations in which men are predominately [sic] active put any real emphasis on structural accommodations to facilitate the involvement of women (day care, car pools, kitchen meetings, etc.).[77]

Some of the organizations had attempted to deal with increasing participation of women in agriculture in an active and positive way. Respondents often spontaneously commented on the quality of the contribution women could make or had made to their organizations. Several referred to the active participation of one or two well-known women — for example, Brigid Pyke of the Canadian Federation of Agriculture.

Most of the respondents, however, felt that it was up to members themselves — and women in particular — to make whatever changes were needed. Few organizations have made an active commitment to increasing women's participation at any level. Rather than recognizing the organizational or structural barriers mentioned by farm women's associations, respondents seemed to focus on women's and men's attitudes.

As mentioned earlier in this section, some studies have suggested that women themselves, through their attitudes, limit their own opportunities to participate. Others focus on women's role in the family, and on unshared domestic responsibilities, rather than on organizational barriers.[78] If these factors contribute significantly to the dilemma, revising membership lists and voting procedures to recognize the spouse, as has been suggested[79] and attempted in some cases,[80] will not be enough. Women themselves must organize to obtain active and effective representation at a variety of levels, and particularly within commodity associations and agencies.

Although the attitudes and prejudices of women and men, and the way that they tend to internalize prescribed gender roles, undoubtedly play a part in limiting women's participation, it is also essential to consider the structural barriers that contribute to the problem (for example, women's lack of transportation, or inability to find evening child care). Furthermore, the effects of apparently fair membership practices that ultimately restrict or limit the participation of entire groups of people should be re-examined.

Consideration of these issues would assist women to identify alternative avenues, and to priorize strategies, according to the circumstances. The possibilities are many. Some, for example, have suggested that "the equal sharing of parenting responsibilities would be a major single factor in freeing farm women for equal participation in farm and community."[81] Other suggestions include development of: rural child-care facilities; special systems for delivering educational programs to women, including assertiveness training; increased rural employment opportunities for women; special outreach programs; changed style, time, or location of meetings; strong women's caucuses within each organization; and comprehensive review of the effects of membership criteria on potential women members.

It is up to farm women themselves, and to all those who profess a concern for equality within the organizations, to begin to develop these strategies. One initial step that women have taken is to organize independently to create a growing number of farm women's organizations.

Farm Women/Women Farmers Organize Independently

Farm women are organizing independently. The voices of women are being heard with clarity and vigour on all aspects of Canadian rural life. Women are forming organizations and acting in concert on many fronts. Farm women's organizations are active in lobbying to affect decisions and legislation that have an impact on themselves and their families. They are developing educational programs for farm wives as well as media campaigns to stimulate awareness of the needs of farm women. They are carrying out research and publishing reports and books. They are also developing strong regional, provincial, and national networks for action and cooperation.

Some women's groups have long played a part in rural life. "Despite some progressive stands on women's rights issues (these) have primarily been an important support network for social contact between farm women and for the sharing of domestic craft skills."[82] Many of the older organizations, however, are also changing to reflect shifts in their membership, and many are beginning to take a more pro-active role in rural life. Other groups have been established more recently. Many of the newer organizations are oriented more to lobbying activities, to addressing issues directly related to the farm sector, and to taking an activist role.

Nevertheless, farm women's organizations share many common goals and objectives. Purely agricultural issues are a principal concern of farm women, as they are of farm men. Issues of farm credit, commodity pricing, returns to investment and labour, and changing financial trends are seen as critical. For example, the Second National Farm Women's Conference in 1985 targetted farm credit and debt issues as its top priority for immediate political action. The growing crisis in farm financing may make these issues even more critical.

Many organizations are also deeply concerned about issues affecting all women, such as child care, legal rights, violence against women, access to credit, and recognition of women's contribution. Farm women, however, have specific needs in relation to these issues, which may differ from those of urban women. For example, while child care in rural communities is at least as essential as it is in urban centres, isolation of many farms and low population density in rural areas create special difficulties and challenges.

Women's position in farm families is also a concern of many organizations. Paid and unpaid farm labour, safety and health hazards, the effects of off-farm work on the family and the enterprise, and growing divorce rates in rural families are some examples of the types of issues being discussed by farm women's organizations. For example, one member of a farm women's organization writes:

> The usual image of farm life is incomplete and unrealistic. The pastoral poetry does not mention that farms have become hazardous places to live; big machinery has produced an accidental death rate on Canadian farms which is 20% higher than the national average.... Rural water supplies do not come from the babbling brook, as depicted by some television shows, but from wells that are endangered by seepage, changes in water table, drilling for oil and gas, and by seismographic testing.[83]

And, one might add, continued heavy use of agricultural chemicals is now starting to take its toll.

Farm women's organizations are also concerned about the issue of quality of rural life, and have identified women's isolation and limited access to services as serious problems: "The declining number of farms and increasing farm size further isolate the farm family as smaller rural communities lose their cohesiveness; and social, educational and commercial services are concentrated in fewer and larger centres."[84] Farm women's extra-long day, and the lack of transportation and mobility, greatly contribute to their isolation.

Farm women's organizations are beginning to challenge the myth of the idyllic life of rural families and to focus attention on the fact that farming is a highly stressful occupation:

> Many do not realize the pressures on the farm family unit and the problems of coping with life on the farm. It is a struggle for the farm family to cope with rising costs of production and unpredictable prices for their products; with the climatic conditions during seed time and harvest; with the time element of activities for both children and adults.... The economic pressure, the decision making, the high seasonal work loads, mounting restrictions, increasing paperwork, family conflict and excessive off-farm activities are all stress factors.[85]

Stress is particularly high for *women* in farm families, partly because, traditionally, she is the family mediator, "not part of the decision-making team . . . (and) she is expected to satisfy all the emotional needs of the family,"[86] and partly also because "the extra long work day eats up the time that urban women take for themselves (for hobbies, books, groups, courses, entertainment, etc.)."[87]

Working together and making common cause as farm women are acknowledged as advantages. One woman eloquently summarizes the potential for concerted action:

> The strength of working together would provide a mechanism to counter-act the present neglected state of farm women. As a unified voice they could lobby for recognition of their contribution to the farm, recognition of pension rights, promotion of policies beneficial to family farming, better roads, better water supply, continuing education or any of the concerns facing them. In effect it would be 'lighting one small candle' as opposed to 'cursing the darkness'.[88]

> Farm women make a significant contribution in the work effort, to the
> financial security, and to the nurturing of the family and the family farm, and
> they do so in an atmosphere devoid of support mechanisms excepting those
> which may occur within the family unit. Governments ignore the contribu-
> tion that farm women make to agricultural production through their
> agricultural policies, lack of benefits and shortage of basic service
> infrastructure. Legal protection for farm women is vague and discrimination
> from lending institutions is prevalent. Society in general and the feminist
> movement in particular have not sufficiently concerned themselves with the
> plight of farm women by not responding to their needs . . . .[89]

Findings reported in this article confirm the first part of this observation.
The agricultural work force is becoming increasingly feminized, as
women become involved in all types of agricultural occupations in
unprecedented numbers. Many more women than ever before are working
as paid employees in agriculture, and women form the large majority of
unpaid family farmworkers. Women have also become more involved in
secondary agricultural occupations. It has been shown, as well, that farm
women are a far from homogeneous group. They can be distinguished
from one another by their relationship to the farm family and to the farm
itself as an enterprise. Some women are operators of farms, many more
are the spouses of operators. One model has been proposed to
characterize the varied and complex contribution that women make to
family agriculture, and the terms *direct involvement*, *indirect support*,
and *direct assistance* were suggested to describe women's contribution on
the farm, in the home, and off the farm. It is important to note that a large
proportion of women are involved in more than one way with the family
farm. Many women work both on and off the farm, as well as in the home.

Despite their extensive involvement, women do not necessarily reap
economic rewards for their labour. Although a mainstay of many family
farms, much of women's labour on farms continues to be unpaid. Those
women who contribute income through off-farm employment do not
appear to become "official" partners in family farms or shareholders in

farm corporations. And women's labour in the home in farm households is likely to be as "invisible" as it is in urban families.

There are other important differences among farm women. Their level of contribution to agriculture is related to a variety of socio-demographic factors, including marital status, age, number and age of children, and education, but also to type of farm organization, level of gross sales, and the commodity produced.

Women's increasingly visible participation in agriculture is reflected in the marked increase in women's enrolment and graduation from agricultural programs in colleges and universities. Unfortunately, this has not yet led to widespread recognition of women's involvement in agriculture, or to modifications of agricultural programs to take women's particular needs into account.

Women are also largely absent from the leadership and even the membership of most farm organizations. Few of these organizations have made any special efforts to recruit or involve women, although almost all appear to recognize that women's participation would be desirable. Many farm women, however, are beginning to organize themselves, to find common issues, to speak out with a united voice on matters of significance to them as farm women, and to attempt to influence policies that affect the well-being and the very survival of farm families.

The analysis of national data presented in this article is only a first step. It is hoped that it will stimulate further investigation of women's involvement in agriculture. It is presented in order to assist and enable women, government policy-makers, and all those concerned with the survival of family farming in Canada to begin to recognize and take into account women's essential contribution in all its dimensions. Policies and practices that will begin to respond to farm women's needs are long overdue.

APPENDIX A

SOME LIMITATIONS OF NATIONAL DATA SOURCES

There are many difficulties with using national census figures to assess the type, nature, and extent of women's contribution to Canadian agriculture.

For example, the census asks whether each individual over 15 years of age in a household worked at all during the last week of May (reference week). Work is defined as not including housework or other work around the home. When a person works more than one job during the week, s/he may be more likely to report the job at which s/he worked the greatest number of hours. Persons with agricultural occupations include farmers, farm managers and foremen, farm labourers, nursery workers, gardeners and grounds-keepers, and others (usually machinery operators and custom workers).

Counting women in agriculture poses several distinct problems. All persons who support the farm through their unpaid work in the home are automatically excluded, thus leaving out much of the essential work that farm women do. Many farm men and women work at full- or part-time jobs off the farm, in addition to working on the farm; however, only one "main" job can be reported. There may be a tendency to report off-farm jobs as their "main" jobs, especially if the farm work is unpaid. (This may be more likely to occur among women.) Therefore, the census provides no way to count the hours that people work on the farm when that work occurs in addition to paid off-farm jobs, as is the case for many farm women. Furthermore, the seasonal nature of agricultural work is such that the need for labour varies over the year. Women often provide this additional seasonal labour in farm families. In many parts of the country, however, May (the month the census forms are filled out by the general population) is not the busiest month on the farm. Both women and men who regularly work on the farm may not work their greatest number of hours in the last week of May.

The census also classifies each individual in one of four possible "classes" of workers. These categories are: self-employed without paid help; self-employed with paid help; unpaid family worker, i.e., working without pay for a relative on a family farm; or paid worker, i.e., family or non-family member who is working for wages, salary, or commission. The 1971 Census inexplicably excluded from the count all *female* farm labourers who were unpaid family workers and worked less than 20 hours per week. The 1981 counts, however, again included all unpaid family workers, regardless of sex.

Another difficulty occurs when using the linked Agriculture and Population Censuses. This linkage creates the category *Census Farm Operator*. The Agriculture Census requests that only one person identify her/himself as the farm operator, defined on the form as the person responsible for making decisions about the farm. This individual is the key person to whom all information about other members of the household from the Population Census is *linked*. Although this simplifies the tabulation of the censuses, it does not necessarily reflect who participates in decision-making on family farms.

MODELS OF WOMEN'S PARTICIPATION ON FAMILY FARMS

The literature suggests that women on family farms can be categorized into different types: the main distinction being whether they work on the farm or off the farm. The following discussion outlines the four main

Figure 5: Women in agriculture: four ways of considering direct involvement and indirect support

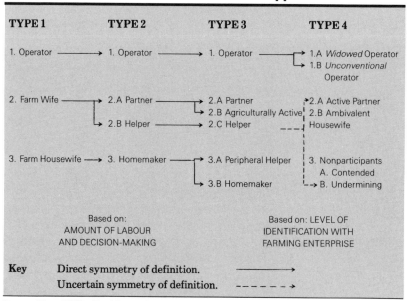

Source: (Type 1) Elise Boulding, "The Labour of U.S. Farm Women: A Knowledge Gap," *Sociology of Work and Occupations*, vol. 7, no. 3 (1979), pp. 261-290.

(Type 2) Jessica Pearson, "Note on Female Farmers," *Rural Sociology*, vol. 44 (February 1979), pp. 189-200.

(Type 3) Dora Lodwick and Polly Fassinger, "Variations in Agriculture Production Activities of Women in Family Farms" (1979), cited in Peggy Ross, "A Commentary on Research on American Farm Women," *Agriculture and Human Values*, vol. 2, no. 1 (1985), pp. 19-30.

(Type 4) Seena Kohl, *Working Together: Women and Family in South Western Saskatchewan* (Toronto: Holt, Rinehart and Winston, 1976).

197

Trying to
measure
women's
contribution
to Canadian
agriculture

models used to consider women's involvement in agriculture. Figure 5 compares the main distinctions and categories used in these models describing farm women's work.

Model 1

The first typology in Figure 5 makes three relatively simple distinctions, classifying farm women as *operators* of farms, *farm wives* (spouses of operators involved in agricultural work), or *farm housewives* (women who are involved solely in household work). These distinctions are based on the degree to which women contribute labour to the operation of the family farm.

Model 2

The second typology is slightly more complex. It maintains the *operator* and *homemaker* distinctions, but further distinguishes between two types of *farm wives*: those who operate the farm jointly with their spouse are called *partners*; those who assist only during peak seasons are termed *helpers*. This distinction recognizes the intermittent and seasonal nature of women's involvement in some types of agricultural activities.

Model 3

The third typology modifies the classifications *partner* and *homemaker* even further, and introduces women's involvement in decision making as an additional basis for classification. The category "partner" is subdivided into three sub-categories, recognizing three different styles of partnership: *partner* (equal partnership); *agriculturally active partner* (women who work on the farm regularly but are not involved in management decisions); and *helper*. The homemaker or farm housewive role is also subdivided. Women who only occasionally contribute labour are represented as *peripheral helpers*. Women who work only in the home retain the title *homemaker*.

Model 4

The fourth typology also is based on degree of involvement in on-farm work and in decision making, but introduces a third factor: the extent to which *farm women* identify with farming. Six distinct groups of farm women are proposed. Two types of operators are recognized: *widowed operators* include women who farm as a result of their partners' death or disability; and *unconventional operators* — women who start farming on their own as a result of inheritance.[90]

Four types of non-operators are identified. Two of these seem similar to the *partner* categories in the previous typologies. Women directly involved in farm work and decision making, and committed to farming, are termed *active partners*. A second type of partner is the *ambivalent housewife*, whose commitment to farming is less strong.

This typology also identifies two types of *non-participants* — a category parallel to the *housewife/homemaker/helper* categories in the previous three typologies. The two non-participant groups are distinguished on the basis of their commitment to the farm: *contented* non-participants are not directly involved in farm work but are happy to live on a farm; *undermining* non-participants are women who want to get out of agriculture. This *undermining* takes the form of being unprepared to put, or to continue to put, the needs of the farm before those of the family and/or discouraging their children's involvement in agriculture.

Discussion/Evaluation

Although the typologies described above can be useful, they have at least three noteworthy weaknesses, and one important omission. Each identifies only two main *groups* of women directly involved in agriculture. As described by the authors, farm women are either operators of the farms or spouses of operators.

The first weakness is in relation to the category *spouse*. Women who are spouses of operators and who work on the farm may, in fact, report themselves, or be reported as, *partners* in the census; they then are classified as *self-employed*. On the other hand, not all spouses may consider themselves, or be considered as, partners in the enterprise and they may not receive a wage or salary; they would then be classified as *unpaid family workers*. Other spouses who receive a wage or salary will be classified as *paid workers*. These distinctions are very important.

Second, another group of farm women is not accounted for at all in the typologies discussed above. This group is only too frequently overlooked, and consists of those women who work in agriculture but have *no familial relationship* to the farm. As hired non-family labour, they have an entirely different relationship to the family farm than do women who are operators or related to operators.

The third weakness of the typologies in Figure 5 relates to the

199

**Trying to
measure
women's
contribution
to Canadian
agriculture**

**Figure 6: Farm women
and men:
Direct
involvement
and/or
assistance**

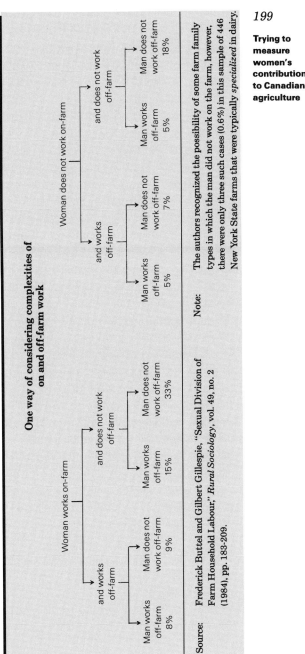

**One way of considering complexities of
on and off-farm work**

Woman works on-farm

and works
off-farm

Man works
off-farm
8%

Man does not
work off-farm
9%

and does not work
off-farm

Man works
off-farm
15%

Man does not
work off-farm
33%

Woman does not work on-farm

and works
off-farm

Man works
off-farm
5%

Man does not
work off-farm
7%

and does not work
off-farm

Man works
off-farm
5%

Man does not
work off-farm
18%

Source: Frederick Buttel and Gilbert Gillespie, "Sexual Division of
Farm Household Labour," *Rural Sociology*, vol. 49, no. 2
(1984), pp. 183-209.

Note: The authors recognized the possibility of some farm family
types in which the man did not work on the farm, however,
there were only three such cases (0.6%) in this sample of 446
New York State farms that were typically *specialized* in dairy.

omission of children's contributions. Children are another group of workers who are typically and frequently overlooked as a source of labour for primary agriculture.[91] Accordingly, the category *other female family members*, both related and unrelated to farm operators, should be included in the definition of women who may be directly involved in agriculture production.

Farm women also contribute to Canadian agriculture from their off-farm work. The typologies discussed above entirely omit this category. Some U.S. studies, which focussed specifically on this form of contribution,[92] have shown that this work is typically undertaken to supplement the income of the farm family, and therefore is a direct contribution to primary agriculture.

The four typologies presented in Figure 5 are based on one fundamental distinction: whether women work on the farm or in the home. The various modifications presented above represent only refinements to these two themes. It has been argued that both types of work — on the farm and in the home — contribute to the economic life of the family farm.[93] The distinction remains important, nevertheless.

Figure 6 illustrates the complexities in a model which includes both the on-farm and the off-farm work of women and men.

As an alternative or in addition to the various models, use of the terms *direct involvement*, *indirect support*, and *direct assistance* to describe various aspects of women's involvement in agriculture is suggested. This terminology is useful because it not only recognizes women's contribution on and off the farm, but permits distinction between the two types of on-farm work. A fuller discussion of these terms is contained in the body of the article.

APPENDIX C

SURVEY OF FARM ORGANIZATIONS: METHOD AND SAMPLE DESCRIPTION

A representative sample was selected from a list of 450 organizations representing or serving Canadian farm families. These included marketing and commodity associations and boards, organizations representing the general or special interests of farmers and farm families, federations of agriculture, retail co-operatives, and credit unions. The sample was chosen to reflect a wide range of types and sizes of organizations, as well as provincial, regional, and national organizations.

Questionnaires were sent to 75 organizations in January 1986. Responses from 78% (58 organizations) were returned; 18% of these were national organizations. The provincial/regional distribution of the remainder was as follows: Maritimes, 8%; Quebec, 16%; Ontario, 16%; Prairies, 44%; British Columbia, 12%; multi-provincial, 4%.

The organizational distribution of the responses was as follows: commodity associations or those that represented various types of producers, 30%; marketing boards or agencies, 26%; farm service organizations, 20%; organizations representing general or particular interests of farm families, 13%; and national or provincial federations of agriculture, 11%.

ORGANIZATIONS SELECTED TO PARTICIPATE IN SURVEY

**Provincial Commodity or
  Marketing Associations or
  Boards** (26)

Nova Scotia Turkey Marketing
  Board
New Brunswick Milk Marketing
  Board
Prince Edward Island Potato
  Marketing Board
Fédération des producteurs de porcs
  du Québec
Fédération des producteurs
  d'agneaux et moutons du Québec
Fédération des producteurs de lait
  du Québec
Ontario Vegetable Growers
  Marketing Board
Ontario Apple Marketing
  Commission
Ontario Pork Producers Marketing
  Board
Ontario Milk Marketing Board
Ontario Fruit and Vegetable
  Growers' Association
Manitoba Beef Commission
Manitoba Chicken Broiler
  Producers' Marketing Board
Manitoba Wheat Pool
Saskatchewan Commercial Egg
  Producers Marketing Board
Saskatchewan Milk Control Board
Saskatchewan Wheat Pool
Alberta Cattle Commission
Alberta Pork Producers Marketing
  Board
Alberta Sugar Beet Growers'
  Marketing Board
Alberta Wheat Pool
British Columbia Fruit Growers'
  Association

British Columbia Grape Marketing
  Board
British Columbia Tree Fruit
  Marketing Board
British Columbia Vegetable
  Marketing Commission
United Grain Growers Limited

**National Commodity or Marketing
  Associations or Boards** (11)

Canadian Cattle Breeders
  Association
Canadian Cattlemen's Association
Canadian Dairy Commission
Canadian Chicken Marketing
  Agency
Canadian Egg Marketing Agency
Canadian Egg Producers Council
Canadian Hatchery Federation
Canadian Pork Council
Canadian Swine Breeders'
  Association
Canadian Turkey Marketing
  Agency
Canadian Wheat Board

**Other National/
  Provincial Organizations** (8)

National Farmers' Union
Quebec Farmers Association
Canadian 4-H Council
Saskatchewan 4-H Council
Canadian Horticultural Association
Canadian Farmers Survival
  Association
Canadian Agricultural Movement
Palliser Wheat Growers Association

203

**Trying to
measure
women's
contribution
to Canadian
agriculture**

Federations of Agriculture (9)

Newfoundland Federation of
    Agriculture
Prince Edward Island Federation of
    Agriculture
Nova Scotia Federation of
    Agriculture
New Brunswick Federation of
    Agriculture Inc.
L'Union des Producteurs Agricoles
    du Québec
Ontario Federation of Agriculture
Unifarm
British Columbia Federation of
    Agriculture
Canadian Federation of Agriculture

Retail and other Co-operatives (11)
Retail: (8)

Coopérative Fédérée
Ontario
Manitoba (2)
Saskatchewan
Alberta
Manitoba (2)

Other (3)

Manitoba Honey Co-operative
Saskatchewan Dairy Producers
    Co-operative
British Columbia Coast Vegetable
    Cooperative Association

Credit Unions (10)

Newfoundland
Prince Edward Island

Nova Scotia
New Brunswick
Confédération des Caisses
    Populaires
Ontario
Manitoba
Saskatchewan
Alberta
British Columbia

1. Sonia Buckmaster, "We are farmers — not farm women," *Western Producer* (December 12, 1985), p. 30.

2. Susan Koski, *The Employment Practices of Farm Women* (Saskatoon: National Farmer's Union, 1982), p. ii.

3. Marjorie Bursa, "Shortage of Farm Labourers," *Agrologist*, vol. 4, no. 2 (1975), p. 21.

4. Frances M. Shaver, "Social Science Research on Farm Women: The State of the Art," *Resources for Feminist Research/Documentation sur la recherche féministe (RFR/DRF)*, vol. 11, no. 1 (March 1982), p. 3.

5. Linda L. Graff, "Industrialization of Agriculture: Implications for the position of women," *Resources for Feminist Research/Documentation sur la recherche féministe (RFR/DRF)*, vol. 11, no. 1 (March 1982), p. 11.

6. Patricia Connelly, *Last Hired, First Fired: Women and the Canadian Work Force* (Toronto: Women's Press, 1978), pp. 103-104.

7. All individuals employed in agricultural occupations in 1981 represent only 62% of those who were so employed in 1951. Of course, this trend is related to the decreasing number of Canadian farms.

8. Joan Farnworth, *Women in Agriculture: what will the new census find?* (Ottawa: Statistics Canada, 1986), 1986 Census of Agriculture, catalogue no. 86.4.1 (27jE).

9. Jac-André Boulet and Laval Lavallée, *The Changing Economic Status of Women*, Economic Council of Canada (Ottawa: Supply and Services Canada, 1984), catalogue no. EC22-122/1984E, p. 46.

10. Canada, Statistics Canada, *Agriculture: A Profile of Canadian Agriculture* (Ottawa: Supply and Services Canada, 1984), 1981 Census of Canada, catalogue no. 96-920, chart 41.

11. Paul Shaw, *Canada's Farm Population: Analysis of Income and Related Characteristics* (Ottawa: Statistics Canada, 1979), catalogue no. 99-750E, p. 92.

12. Farnworth, *Women in Agriculture.*

13. Canada, Statistics Canada, "Unpublished tabulations from Agriculture Population Linkage," 1981 Census of Canada.

14. *Ibid.*

15. Koski, *The Employment Practices of Farm Women*, 1982, p. 33.

16. Canada, Labour Canada, Women's Bureau, *Women in The Labour Force. Part 1 Participation* (Ottawa: Supply and Services Canada, 1983), catalogue no. L. 38-30/1983-1, p. 47.

17. *Ibid.*, p. 47.

18. *Ibid.*, p. 55.

19. Polly Fassinger and Harry Schwarzweller, *Exploring Women's Work Roles on Family Farms: a Michigan Case Study*, cited in Peggy Ross, "A Commentary on Research on American Farm Women," *Agriculture and Human Values*, vol. 2, no. 1 (1985), p. 24.

20. Nora Cebotarev, W.M. Blacklock, and L. McIsaac, "Farm Women's Work Patterns," *Atlantis*, vol. 11, no. 2 (spring 1986), pp. 1-22.

21. Koski, *The Employment Practices of Farm Women*, p. 32.

22. Cebotarev, Blacklock, and McIsaac, "Farm Women's Work Patterns," 1986.

23. Bill Reimer, "Women as Farm Labour," *Rural Sociology*, vol. 51, no. 2 (1986), table 3.

24. *Ibid.*, p. 9.

25. Koski, *The Employment Practices of Farm Women*, p. 33.

26. Reimer, "Women as Farm Labour," table 2.

27. Pat and Hugh Armstrong, *The Double Ghetto: Canadian Women and their Segregated Work* (Toronto: McClelland and Stewart, 1984).

Meg Luxton, *More Than a Labour of Love: Three Generations of Women's Work in the Home* (Toronto: Women's Press, 1980).

28. Seena Kohl, *Working Together: Women and Family in South Western Saskatchewan* (Toronto: Holt, Rinehart and Winston, 1976), p. 67.

29. J.L. Swinamer, "The Value of Household Work in Canada, 1981," *Canadian Statistical Review*, vol. 60, no. 3 (March 1985), catalogue no. 11-003E, pp. vi-xiv.

30. Robert O. Blood, Jr., "The Division of Labour in City and Farm Families," *Marriage and Family Living*, vol. 20, no. 2 (May 1958), pp. 170-174.

31. Norah Keating and Maryanne Doherty, *An Analysis of the Farm Production Unit with*

Recommendations for Improving Net Farm Income (Edmonton: University of Alberta, Home Economics Faculty, 1985), table 15.

32. Koski, *The Employment Practices of Farm Women*, p. 29.

33. Dion, *Les femmes dans l'agriculture au Québec* (Longueuil, Quebec: les éditions La Terre de chez-nous, 1983).

34. Keating and Doherty, 1985, p. 35.

35. Koski, *The Employment Practices of Farm Women*, p. 31.

36. *Ibid*, pp. 25 and 35.

37. Dion, *Les femmes dans l'agriculture au Québec*.

38. Koski, *The Employment Practices of Farm Women*, p. 29.

39. Frederick Buttel and Gilbert Gillespie, "The Sexual Division of Farm Household Labour: An Exploratory Study of the Structure of On-Farm and Off-Farm Labor Allocation Among Farm Men and Women," *Rural Sociology*, vol. 49, no. 2 (1984), p. 199.

40. If women with agricultural occupations are excluded from the total, census figures show that women in clerical, sales, and service occupations comprised 57.31% of the female labour force in 1981. Canada, Statistics Canada, *Population: Labour force — occupation trends* (Ottawa: Supply and Services Canada, 1983), 1981 Census of Canada, catalogue no. 92-920, table 1.

41. *Second National Farm Women's Conference Proceedings*, Charlottetown, P.E.I., November 21-24, 1985.

42. Barbara Sawer, "Predictors of Farm Wife's Involvement in General

Management and Adoption Decisions," *Rural Sociology*, vol. 38, no. 4 (winter 1973), p. 422.

43. *Ibid.*, p. 424.

44. Gisele Ireland, *The Farmer Takes a Wife* (Chesley, Ontario: Concerned Farm Women, 1983), p. 15.

45. Dion, *Les femmes dans l'agriculture au Québec*, pp. 46-49.

46. L.M. McIsaac, "The Role of Women in the Operation of Family Farms in Prince Edward Island," Masters Thesis, University of Guelph, 1983.

47. Valda Gillis, "Prince Edward Island Farm Women and Off-Farm Employment," excerpt from *Structure of Maritime (Periphery) Agriculture with Specific Reference to Farm Women and the Role of Off-Farm Income*, Masters Thesis, University of Guelph, 1985.

48. *Ibid.*

49. *Ibid.*

50. *Ibid.*

51. McIsaac, "The Role of Women in the Operation of Family Farms in Prince Edward Island."

52. *Ibid.*

53. Canada, Statistics Canada, *Agriculture: Canada* (Ottawa: Supply and Services Canada, 1982), 1981 Census of Canada, catalogue no. 96-901, p. vii.

54. Canada, Statistics Canada, *Agriculture: Canada* (1978), table 1.

Canada, Statistics Canada, *Agriculture: Canada* (1983), table 35.

55. Ross, "A Commentary on Research on American Farm Women," p. 28.

56. Buttel and Gillespie, "The Sexual Division of Farm Household Labour," p. 196.

57. Canada, Statistics Canada, "Unpublished Tabulations from the Agriculture Population Linkage."

58. Ray D. Bollman and Pamela Smith, "Integration of Canadian Farm and Off-Farm Markets and the Off-Farm Work Participation Patterns of Farm Women, Men and Children," table 2.

59. Philip Ehrensaft and Ray D. Bollman, "Structure and Concentration in Canadian Agriculture: A Micro-analysis of the Census of Agriculture," presented to Canadian Sociology and Anthropology Association annual meeting, Vancouver, 1983, table 4.

60. Farnworth, *Women in Agriculture: What Will the New Census Find?*

61. Canada, Dominion Bureau of Statistics, *Labour Force Occupations by Sex, Canada and Provinces* (Ottawa: Queen's Printer and Controllor of Stationery, 1963), 1961 Census of Canada, catalogue no. 94-503, table 6.

Canada, Statistics Canada, *Population*, table 1.

62. "Young Women are Now Returning Home to the Farm," *Contact*, vol. 11, no. 2 (1985), published by Kemptville College of Agricultural Technology, p. 1.

63. G.E. Laliberté, "Canadian Agriculture Programs: Trends in Enrollment," *Agrologist*, vol. 11, no. 1 (1982), pp. 6-9.

F.L. McEwen and G.L. Brinkham, "The Role of Education and Research," in *Farming and The Rural Community in Ontario: An Introduction*, ed. T. Fuller (Toronto: Foundation for Rural Living, 1984), pp. 101-120.

64. Richard Barichello, *A Profile of Human Resources in British Columbia Agriculture*, prepared for Agriculture Canada, Regional Development Branch (New Westminster, British Columbia: The Branch, 1985).

Edward B. Harvey and John H. Blakely, *Demand and Supply for Agricultural Professionals in Canada: Executive Summary* (Ottawa: Agricultural Institute of Canada, 1985).

65. Bursa, "Shortage of Farm Labourers," p. 21.

66. Margrit Eichler and Jeanne Lapointe, *On the Treatment of the Sexes in Research* (Ottawa: Social Sciences and Humanities Research Council of Canada, 1985).

67. Boulet and Lavallée, *The Changing Economic Status of Women*, p. 27.

68. *Ibid.*, p. 28.

69. *Ibid.*, p. 4.

70. Women for the Survival of Agriculture, *What Are You Worth? A Study of the Economic Contribution of Eastern Ontario Farm Women to the Family Farm Enterprise*, presented at the Second National Farm Women Conference, Charlottetown, P.E.I., November 21-24, 1985, p. 47.

71. Norma Taylor, "All This for Three and a Half a Day," in *Women in the Canadian Mosaic*, ed. Gwen Matheson (Toronto: Peter Matheson Associates, 1976), p. 162.

72. Research, Action and Education Centre, "Keeping Women Down on the Farm," *Resources for Feminist Research/Documentation sur la recherche féministe (RFR/DRF)*, vol. 11, no. 1 (March 1982), pp. 12-14.

73. Suzanne Dion and Giselle Painchaud, "La participation des femmes dans la vie syndicale agricole," *Resources for Feminist Research/Documentation sur la recherche féministe (RFR/DRF)*, vol. 11, no. 1 (March 1982), pp. 7-8.

74. Research, Action and Education Centre, "Keeping Women Down on the Farm," p. 13.

75. Taylor, "All This for Three and a Half a Day," p. 162.

76. Molly McGhee, *Women in Rural Life: The Changing Scene* (Toronto: Ministry of Food and Agriculture, 1984), p. 24.

77. Research, Action and Education Centre, "Keeping Women Down on the Farm," p. 14.

78. Dion and Painchaud, "La participation des femmes dans la vie syndicale agricole," p. 7.

79. Women for the Survival of Agriculture, *What Are You Worth?*, p. 47.

80. Research, Action and Education Centre, *"Keeping Women Down on the Farm,"* p. 14.

81. *Ibid.*.

82. *Ibid.*

83. Leda Jensen, "Stress in the Farm Family Unit," *Resources for Feminist Research/Documentation sur la recherche féministe (RFR/DRF)*, vol. 11, no. 1 (March 1982), p. 12.

84. Research, Action and Education Centre, "Keeping Women Down on the Farm," p. 13.

85. Jensen, "Stress in the Farm Family Unit," p. 11.

86. *Ibid.*, p. 12.

87. Research, Action and Education
Centre, "Keeping Women Down on
the Farm," p. 13.

88. Koski, *The Employment Practices of
Farm Women*, p. 54.

89. *Ibid.*

90. The term "unconventional" refers to
community standards and norms.
These are women who have "rejected
the traditional set of expectations
for women in the region." Kohl,
*Working Together: Women and
Family in South Western
Saskatchewan*, p. 106.

91. Max Hedley, "Normal Expectations:
Rural Women Without Property,"
*Resources for Feminist
Research/Documentation sur la
recherche féministe (RFR/DRF)*, vol.
11, no. 1 (March 1982), pp. 15-17.

S.C. Farrier, J.M. Maxwell, and J.K.
Newhouse, "The Role of the Child in
the Family Farm," paper presented
to the Southern Association of
Agricultural Scientists Annual
Meeting, Atlanta, Georgia, 1983.

92. Janet Bokemeier, Verna Keith, and
Carolyn Sachs, *What Happened to
Rural Women? A Comparative
Study of Labour Force Participation*,
cited in Peggy Ross, "A
Commentary on Research on
American Farm Women," p. 24.

93. Fassinger and Schwarzweller,
*Exploring Women's Work Roles on
Family Farms: a Michigan Case
Study*, cited in Peggy Ross, "A
Commentary on Research on
American Farm Women," p. 24.

Selected Bibliography
and
Audio-Visual References

210

Selected
bibliography
and
audio-visual
references

SELECTED BIBLIOGRAPHY AND AUDIO-VISUAL REFERENCES

Canadian Agriculture

1. Canada. Statistics Canada. *Agriculture: A Profile of Canadian Agriculture*. Ottawa: Supply and Services Canada, 1984 (1981 Census of Canada, catalogue no. 96-920).

2. Canada. Statistics Canada, Structural Analysis Division, Analytical Studies Branch. *Human Activity and the Environment: A Statistical Compendium*. Ottawa: Supply and Services Canada, 1986 (catalogue no. 11-509E).

3. Canada. Task Force on Program Review, Study Team. *Agriculture. Economic Growth Series*. Ottawa: Supply and Services Canada, 1985.

4. Giangrande, Carole. *Down to Earth: The Crisis in Canadian Farming*. Toronto: House of Anasi Press, 1985.

5. Sage Knell, Irene and John R. English. *Canadian Agriculture in a Global Context: Opportunities and Obligations*. Waterloo, Ontario: University of Toronto Press, 1986.

6. *La Terre de chez nous*. Longueuil, Quebec: Union des producteurs agricoles (UPA), 1929-.

7. *The Western Producer: A Weekly Newspaper Serving Western Canadian Farmers*. Saskatoon: Saskatchewan Wheat Pool, 1923-.

The Contribution of Women to Agriculture

1. Dion, Suzanne. *Les femmes dans l'agriculture au Québec*. Longueuil, Quebec: Les éditions La Terre de chez nous, 1983.

2. *Farm Women*. Winnipeg: Farm Women, 1983-. Note: previous title: *Canadian Farm Women*.

3. *First National Farm Women's Conference Background Papers*. Ottawa, December 2-4, 1980.

4. Ireland, Gisele. *The Farmer Takes a Wife*. Chesley, Ontario: Concerned Farm Women, 1983.

5. Koski, Susan. *The Employment Practices of Farm Women*. Saskatoon: National Farmers Union, 1982.

6. McGhee, Molly. *Women in Rural Life: The Changing Scene*. Toronto: Ministry of Agriculture and Food, 1984.

7. *Resources for Feminist Research / Documentation sur la recherche féministe (RFR / DRF). Women in Agriculture and Rural Society/les femmes dans la production agricole et la societé rurale* (thematic issue), ed. Nora Cebotarev, and Frances Shaver, vol. 11, no. 1, March 1982.

8. Rose-Lizée, Ruth. *Portrait des femmes collaboratrices du Québec*. Saint-Lambert: Association des femmes collaboratrices du Québec, 1984.

9. *Second National Farm Women's Conference Proceedings.* Charlottetown, Prince Edward Island, November 21-24, 1985.

10. Women for the Survival of Agriculture. *What Are You Worth?: A Study of the Economic Contribution of Eastern Ontario Farm Women to the Family Farm Enterprise.* Submitted to the Second National Farm Women's Conference, Charlottetown, Prince Edward Island, November 21-24, 1985.

The Role of Women in the North American Agricultural System

1. Alberta Agriculture. Home Economics Branch. *Partners in Agriculture: The Farm Wife's Economic Contribution to the Agricultural Business.* Edmonton, Alberta: Alberta Agriculture, 1983 (Homedex 1830-11).

2. Barthez, Alice. *Famille, travail et agriculture.* Paris: Economica, 1982.

3. Bescher, Donnelly L. and L.W. Smith. "The Changing Roles and Status of Rural Women." In *The Family in Rural Society.* Ed. R.T. Coward and Willm. Jr. Smith. Boulder, Colorado: Westview Press, 1981.

4. Binnie-Clark, Georgina. *Wheat and Women.* Toronto: University of Toronto Press, 1979.

5. Blood, Robert, O., Jr. "The Division of Labour in City and Farm Families." *Marriage and Family Living*, vol. 20, no. 2 (May 1958), pp. 170-174.

6. Bollman, R.D. "Who are the Farmers?". *Canadian Journal of Agricultural Economics*, vol. 31, 1983, pp. 1-13.

7. Buttel, Frederick H. and Gilbert W. Gillespie. "The Sexual Division of Farm Household Labour: An Exploratory Study of the Structure of On-Farm and Off-Farm Labor Allocation among Farm Men and Women." *Rural Sociology*, vol. 49, no. 2, 1984, pp. 183-209.

8. Canada. Agriculture Canada. *Women: a Driving Force in the Agri-Food System.* Ottawa: Agriculture Canada, 1983 (publication no. 5176B).

9. Council on Rural Development Canada. *Rural Women: their Work, their Needs and their Role in Rural*

212

Development. Ottawa: Supply and Services Canada, 1979 (catalogue no. RE 41-5/1979).

10. Dion, Suzanne. "The Effects of the Agriculture Crisis on the Farm Woman's Family and her Rural Community". In *Second National Farm Women's Conference Proceedings.* Charlottetown, Prince Edward Island, November 21-24, 1985.

11. Dumas, Marie-Claire. "S.O.S. des femmes de terre." *Châtelaine*, vol. 26, no. 4, April 1985, p. 136 et seq.

12. Hedley, Max. "Relations of Production on the Family Farm: Canadian Prairies." *The Journal of Peasant Studies*, vol. 9, no. 1, 1981, pp. 71-85.

13. Kohl, Seena B. "Women's Participation in the North American Family Farm." *Women's Studies International Quarterly*, vol. 1, no. 1, 1978, pp. 47-54.

14. _____ . *Working Together: Women and Family in South Western Saskatchewan.* Toronto: Holt, Rinehart and Winston, 1976.

15. Lipkin, Mary Jane, co-ordinator, Status of Rural Women Project. "The Invisible Pitch Fork or The Portrayal of Farm Women in the Canadian Media." *First National Farm Women's Conference Background Papers.* Ottawa, December 2-4, 1980.

16. McIsaac, Leona Marie. "The Role of Women in the Operation of Family Farms in Prince Edward Island." Masters Thesis, University of Guelph, 1983.

17. Rosenfeld, Rachel Ann. *Farm Women Work, Farm and the Family in the United States.* Chapel Hill, N.C.: University of North Carolina Press, 1985.

18. Rosenfeld, Stuart A., ed. *Brakeshoes, Backhoes and Balance Sheets: The Changing Vocational Education of Rural Women.* Washington, D.C.: Rural American Women Inc., 1981.

19. Ross, Peggy. "A Commentary on Research on American Farm Women." *Agriculture and Human Values*, vol. 2, no. 1, 1985, pp. 19-30.

20. Sachs, Carolyn. *The Invisible Farmers: Women in Agricultural Production.* Totowa, N.J.: Rowman and Allanheld, 1983.

21. Salant, Priscilla. *Farm Women: Contribution to Farm and Family.* Washington, D.C.: U.S. Department of Agriculture. Economic Research Service. Economic Development Division; Mississipi Agricultural and Forestry Experiment Station. Department of Agricultural Economics, 1983 (Agricultural Economics Research Report no. 140).

22. Saskatchewan Department of Labour. Women's Division. *Farm Women.* Regina, Sask.: 1977.

23. Sawer, Barbara. "Predictors of the Farm Wife's Involvement in General Management and Adoption Decisions." *Rural Sociology*, vol. 38, no. 4, 1973, pp. 412-426.

24. _____ . *The Role of the Wife in Farm Decisions.* Vancouver: University of British Columbia. Adult Education Research Centre, 1974 (Rural Sociology Monograph no. 5).

25. Scholl, K. "Classification of Women as Farmers: Economic Implications." *Family Economics Review*, vol. 4, 1983, pp. 10-15.

26. _____ . "Farm Women's Triad of Roles." *Family Economics Review*, vol. 1, 1983, pp. 10-15.

27. Shaver, Frances. "Social Science Research on Farm Women: The State of the Art." *Resources for Feminist Research /Documentation sur la recherche féministe (RFR/DRF)*, vol. 11, no. 1, March 1982, pp. 3-4.

28. Trottier, Mariette. "La situation économique des productrices agricoles au Québec." Masters Thesis, Université du Québec à Montréal (UQUAM), 1984.

Audio-Visual References

Distributed by the National Film Board (NFB).

> *Potatoes*
> *(La ferme familiale en danger)*
> 27 minutes, 28 seconds
> 1976
> Director: Robert Lang
> Producers: Gary Toole, Roman Bittman, Colin Low

Summary: This documentary deals with the gradual shift from the family farm to corporation-run farms, with all the ensuing problems and personal hardship. It is an incisive evaluation of what is happening in North American and world-wide agriculture today.

Produced by the NFB for the Canadian International Development Agency.

> *Growing Dollars*
> *(La récolte des dollars)*
> 28 minutes, 52 seconds
> 1978
> Director: Tina Viljoen
> Producer: Barrie Howells

Summary: The Green Revolution, which caused the dramatic increase in grain production during the mid-1960s, was an important agricultural advance in many Third World countries. But it has had wide repercussions on all types of farming. Large-scale mechanized farms began to take over smaller farms, forcing small and tenant farmers — who lost their land — to migrate to the cities, where they now swell the ranks of the urban unemployed. This is a look at "agribusiness," a term to describe the multinational corporations that are attempting to create a world agricultural system in which everything they produce is for consumers in the already-wealthy countries.

Produced by the Canadian Broadcasting Corporation (CBC).

> *Food for Thought* (available in English only)
> 56 minutes, 37 seconds
> 1979

Summary: Forced to compete against low-priced imported fresh fruit and vegetables, Canadian farmers are feeling the pressure of expanding agricultural production. Are Canadian farmers on the verge of bankruptcy? This documentary examines the problems facing the Canadian fruit and vegetable industry from a number of angles.

Produced by the NFB for the Challenge for Change/Société nouvelle program, in cooperation with Canadian government departments and agencies.

> *De grâce et d'embarras* (available in French only)
> 94 minutes, 10 seconds
> 1979
> Director: Marcel Carrière
> Producer: Jacques Gagné

Summary: The daily lives of a farmer who is the last resident of an island in the St. Lawrence River and a muskrat hunter living on another island nearby bring to light the contradictions of a way of living altered by the city.

Distributed by the NFB.

Les enfants du Gumbo (available in French only)
72 minutes, 51 seconds
1982
Director: Michel Régnier
Producer: René Piché

Summary: This film is a family portrait of the people of the Peace River District, a farming region in northern Alberta. It looks at the efforts of this Franco-Albertan community to maintain the delicate balance between success in farming operations and preservation, even enhancement, of an increasingly endangered French cultural heritage.

Produced by the NFB, Studio D, in association with Pacific Region production.

This Borrowed Land (available in English only)
28 minutes, 49 seconds
1984
Director: Bonnie Kreps
Producers: Signe Johansson, Kathleen Shannon

Summary: The Peace River Valley in British Columbia is an area of rich farmland threatened by the construction of a hydro-electric dam. This film gives the women who farm the Peace the chance to voice their growing concern over the conversion of farmland to uses not related to the production of food. They ask: "Will we leave our children enough land to grow food on?" They are firmly committed to their lifestyle despite the difficulties, both concrete and imponderable. A film about agriculture, ecology, land misuse, and the stout-willed farmers who happen to be women.

Women Farmworkers in Non-familial Businesses

1. Bains, Amar. "Conditions of Farm Work: by a Woman Farm Worker as told to Amar Bains." *Resources for Feminist Research / Documentation sur la recherche féministe (RFR /DRF)*, vol. 11, no. 1, March 1982, pp. 5-6.

2. Borst, John et al. *Legal Resource Book for Farm and Domestic Workers*. Yarrow, B.C.: Labour Advocacy and Research Association (LARA), 1977.

3. Canadian Advisory Council on the Status of Women. *Women in Agriculture* (fact sheet). Ottawa: 1985.

4. Cavanagh, Judy. "The Plight of Women Farmworkers." *Resources for Feminist Research / Documentation sur la recherche féministe (RFR/DRF)*, vol. 11, no. 1, March 1982, pp. 6-7.

5. Graff, Linda L. "The Changing Nature of Farm Women's Work Roles Under the Industrialization of Agricultural Production." Masters Thesis, McMaster University, 1979.

6. Harasim, Linda and Lucio Teles. *Farmworkers: the Invisible Minority in Ontario: an Introduction for the Public*. Toronto: Tolpuddle Farm Labour Information Centre, 1983.

7. Holt, James S. "Introduction to the Seasonal Farm Labour Problem." In *Seasonal Agricultural Labour Markets in the United States*. Ed. Robert D. Emerson. Ames, Iowa: Iowa State University Press, 1984, pp. 3-32.

8. Sharma, Hari. "Race and Class in British Columbia: the Case of B.C.'s Farmworkers." *South Asia Bulletin*, vol. 3, no. 1, spring 1983, pp. 53-60.

Audio-Visual References

Distributed by the National Film Board (NFB).

> The Back-Breaking Leaf
> (La feuille qui brise les reins)
> 29 minutes, 30 seconds
> 1959, black and white
> Director: Terence
> Macartney-Filgate
> Producers: Roman Kroitor,
> Wolf Koenig, Tom Daly

Summary: Smokers say it's relaxing, but tobacco harvesters call it "the back-breaking leaf." Here is a graphic picture of the tobacco harvest in southwestern Ontario, presented from the points of view of the transient field workers who move in for a brief bonanza when the leaves are ripe, and of the farmers who depend solely on this crop.

Distributed by the NFB.

> On the Tobacco Road
> (Les gars du tabac)
> 26 minutes, 3 seconds
> 1977
> Director: Maurice Bulbulian
> Producer: Jean-Marc Garand

Summary: The tobacco fields around Delhi, Ontario, attract hordes of young pickers, many of whom come from Quebec. This year, work is scarce. Rumour has it that foreign — and cheaper — migrant labour has been imported. The Québecois gather in the town's parks, waiting for jobs. The camera singles out a group of them, and shows their experiences at the hands of the law, and a group of racist hoodlums.

Distributed by the NFB.

215

Selected
bibliography
and
audio-visual
references

> A Time to Rise (available in
> English only)
> 39 minutes, 45 seconds
> 1981
> Directors/Producers: Anand
> Patwardhan, Jim Monro

Summary: On April 6, 1980, the Canadian Farmworkers Union came into existence. This film documents the conditions that provoked the formation of the union, and the response of growers and labour contractors to the threat of unionization. Made over a period of two years, the film is eloquent testimony to the progress of the workers' movement from the first stirrings of militancy to the energetic canvassing of union members.

> To Pick is Not to Choose
> 44 minutes
> 1985
> Producers: John Greyson and Toni
> Venturi (for the Tolpuddle Farm
> Labour Information Committee)

Summary: Filmed during the 1984 harvest, this documentary examines the experiences of four female farmworkers in southwestern Ontario. Their stories outline their problems, especially the very bad working conditions.

The Judicial and Economic Status of Women in Agriculture

1. Association féminine d'éducation et d'action sociale (AFEAS). "The Wife Contributing with her Husband to an Enterprise for Profit: Revised Recommendations, September 1979." *First National Farm Women's Conference Background Papers*. Ottawa, December 2-4, 1980.

2. Barthez, Alice. "Le travail familial et les rapports de domination dans l'agriculture." *Nouvelles questions féministes*, no. 5, 1983, pp. 19-46.

3. Desjardins, Micheline. *On ne compte pas! Dossier socio-économique sur la situation des femmes collaboratrices dans les Prairies*. Ottawa: Fédération des femmes canadiennes-françaises, 1984.

4. Dulude, Louise. *Love, Marriage and Money. . . An Analysis of Financial Relations Between the Spouses*. Ottawa: Canadian Advisory Council on the Status of Women, 1984.

5. Lipkin, Mary Jane, co-ordinator, Status of Rural Women Project. "Equal Partner or 'Just a Wife': Farm Wives and Property Law in Canada." *First National Farm Women's Conference Background Papers*. Ottawa, December 2-4, 1980.

6. Lipkin, Mary Jane, co-ordinator, Status of Rural Women Project. "Old MacDonald had a Farm: But Will his Son or Daughter? Government Policies Promoting Young Farmers." *First National Farm Women's Conference Background Papers*. Ottawa, December 2-4, 1980.

7. Lipkin, Mary Jane, co-ordinator, Status of Rural Women Project. "Credit Where Credit is Due: Women and Farm Credit in Canada." *First National Farm Women's Conference Background Papers*. Ottawa, December 2-4, 1980.

8. McLeod, Carol. "Shadow of the Eight Ball: Women and Credit in Canada." *Rights and Freedoms*, no. 56, summer 1985, pp. 13-15.

9. Meanwell, Catherine and Susan Glover. *"To Have and to Hold" — A Guide to Property and Credit Law for Farm Families in Ontario*. Chesley, Ontario: Concerned Farm Women, 1984.

10. Quebec. Ministère du Conseil exécutif, Secrétariat à la condition féminine, Groupe de travail sur la déclaration de statut de la femme collaboratrice. *Femmes collaboratrices: un statut à choisir*. Quebec: Secrétariat à la condition féminine, 1986.

11. Quebec. Ministère du Conseil exécutif, Secrétariat à la condition féminine. *The Government's Action Plan in Matters Concerning the Status of Women 1986-1987*. Quebec: Secrétariat à la condition féminine, 1986.

12. Steel, Freda M. "The Ideal Marital Property Regime — What Would It Be?" In *Family Law in Canada: New Directions*. Ed. Elizabeth Sloss. Ottawa: Canadian Advisory Council on the Status of Women, 1985, pp. 127-169.

Audio-Visual References

Produced by the NFB with the participation of the Women's Program, Secretary of State.

> *Plenty of Nothing
> (Madame, vous avez rien)*
> 55 minutes, 55 seconds
> 1982
> Director: Dagmar Gueissaz
> Producer: Jacques Vallée

Summary: Half a million wives work with their husbands in family-run businesses, but most have no legal title to any part of the operation. This documentary focusses on several farm wives who are seeking their fair share of the family farm. In frank and friendly discussions with their husbands and with financial advisers, the women learn about co-ownership. The importance of having a legal arrangement becomes clear when a former farm wife tells how she lost everything she thought she owned when she and her husband divorced. Filmed in Quebec's fertile Richelieu Valley, this film encourages women to recognize the economic value of their work and to seek the legal recognition of their status and of their right to an equitable financial share. An English version of a French original.

Co-produced by NFB, Prairie Region, and CBC.

Change of Heart (available in English only)
56 minutes, 28 seconds
1984
Director: Anne Wheeler
Producers: Anne Frank, Tom Radford, Sig Gerber

Summary: This film is a compassionate drama about the disintegration of a loveless marriage. Edna and Bob (sensitively played by Joy Coghill and Ken James) have spent all their married life working on their Alberta farm. After 30 years, no longer willing to tolerate Bob's hostility and bullying, Edna packs her bags. Her decision to leave her husband and build a new life throws the family into an uproar and brings dramatically into focus the issue of a farm wife's right to a share of the family gains, and the problems associated with mid-life divorce and older women's re-entry into the work force.

The Needs and Resources of Women in Agriculture

1. Benedict, Ruth. "Sorry, No Kids Allowed." *Farm Women News*, September 1985, p. 17.

2. Boisseau, Peter R. "Farmer's Lung: It's finally being diagnosed by New Brunswick doctors." *The Times-Transcript*, vol. 2, no. 239, October 1983, p. 1.

3. Canada. Task Force on Child Care. *Report of the Task Force on Child Care*. Ottawa: Supply and Services Canada, 1986.

4. Craig, Linda. "Factors associated with Stress in Farm Women." Presented to the Canadian Sociology and Anthropology Association, Learned Societies Conference, University of Guelph, June 6-9, 1984.

5. Davis, Ellen and Ellen Olechowski. *Women in Rural Life Education: Study Conducted at St. Clair College of Applied Arts and Technology*. Windsor, Ontario: St. Clair College of Applied Arts and Technology, 1985.

6. Dion, Suzanne. "Les besoins de formation professionnelle des agricultrices". Masters Thesis, University of Montreal, 1985.

7. Fochs Heller, Anita. *Health and Home: Women as Health Guardians*. Ottawa: Canadian Advisory Council on the Status of Women, 1986.

8. Harkin, Dianne. "Who's Minding the Kids?". *Canada Poultryman*, vol. 71, no. 10, October 1984, pp. 42-43.

9. Hundertmark, Susan. "Rural Feminism." *Healthsharing*, vol. 7, no. 1, winter 1985, pp. 14-17.

10. Manitoba Advisory Council on the Status of Women. *Some Concerns of Rural and Farm Women*. Winnipeg: 1984.

218

**Selected
bibliography
and
audio-visual
references**

11. Miller Chenier, Nancy. *Reproductive Hazards at Work: Men, Women and the Fertility Gamble*. Ottawa: Canadian Advisory Council on the Status of Women, 1982.

12. Nesbitt, Darell. "Farm Women Learn Farming Techniques." *Shoal Lake Star*, March 19, 1986, p. 9.

13. Ontario Task Force on Health and Safety in Agriculture. *Report*. Toronto: Ministry of Agriculture and Food; Ministry of Labour, 1985.

14. Quebec. Ministère de l'Agriculture, des Pêcheries et de l'Alimentation. Bureau de la répondante à la condition féminine. *From Sharing the Work to Sharing the Power: Three Year Plan*. Quebec: 1986.

15. Ross, Lois, L. "Farm Women: The Unrecognized Resource." In *Prairie Lives: The Changing Face of Farming*. Toronto: Between the Lines, 1985.

16. Sweet, Lois. "Voices of Rural Women Heard at Last." *Toronto Star*, July 7, 1984, p. L3.

17. Wellington Rural Child Care Network. *Proceedings from Working for Change*; October 4, 1985. Guelph, Ontario: University of Guelph, 1985.

18. Women of Unifarm. *Coping with Stress on the Farm*. Edmonton, Alberta: 1979.

19. _____ . *Perceptions of Farm Women: Final Report*. Edmonton, Alberta: 1984.

20. _____ . *Stresses in the Farm Family Unit*. Edmonton, Alberta: 1978.

Audio-Visual References

Distributed by the NFB.

> *Play Safe* (available in English only)
> 27 minutes, 30 seconds
> 1978
> Director/Producer: Brian M. Chadderton

Summary: As part of the "play safe program" of the War Amputations of Canada Association, children and young adolescents tell stories of childhood accidents that have caused them to lose arms or legs. Showing their prostheses and describing in matter-of-fact fashion the details of their accidents (playing near farm machinery, train tracks, snow removal equipment, or lawn mowers), the safety message to both parents and children is a powerful one. For purchase, contact The War Amputations of Canada.

Produced by Studio D of the NFB.

> *A Safe Distance* (available in English only)
> 28 minutes
> 1986

Summary: This film looks at various services and programs designed to meet the special needs of women in rural, northern, and native communities. The film introduces a group of women in Portage La Prairie, Manitoba, who set up a Safe House project because they felt the need for a confidential approach to providing shelters for battered women and their children. The women of West Bay Reserve in Ontario chose instead to construct a large shelter to stand as a visible reminder that women will no longer tolerate violence at the hands of men in the community.

The film examines these and other innovative approaches to providing much-needed services to battered women

in isolated areas. It introduces the
women who worked to establish these
services, often with very little resources,
in communities holding rigid, traditional
attitudes toward the woman's place in
the family.

219

**Selected
bibliography
and
audio-visual
references**

The Canadian Advisory Council on the Status of Women was established as an independent advisory body in 1973 in response to a recommendation by the Royal Commission on the Status of Women. Its mandate, "to bring before the government and the public matters of interest and concern to women" and "to advise the Minister on such matters relating to the status of women as the Minister may refer to the Council for its consideration or as the Council may deem appropriate", is wide and may be interpreted to cover all Council activities on behalf of Canadian women.

The Council is an autonomous agency that reports to Parliament through the Minister Responsible for the Status of Women. This allows the Council to maintain a voice within Parliament and at the same time maintain the right to publish without ministerial consent.

The following were members of the Canadian Advisory Council on the Status of Women at the time of publication (1987):

Sylvia Gold
President
Ottawa, Ontario

Patricia Cooper
Vice-President
Calgary, Alberta

Clarisse Codère
Vice-President
Montreal, Quebec

Monique Bernard
Mont St-Hilaire, Que.

Myriam B. Bernstein
Montreal, Quebec

Erminie Joy Cohen
Saint John, N.B.

Shanon Louise Cooper
Mayo, Yukon

Jo-Ann Cugnet
North Battleford, Sask.

Héleyne D'Aigle
Edmundston,
New Brunswick

Edith Daly
Montague, P.E.I.

Lawrie Montague Edinboro
Chatham, Ontario

Marthe Gill
Pointe Bleue, Quebec

Alison Hinchey
New Waterford, Nova Scotia

Darlene Julianne Hincks
Regina, Saskatchewan

Veronica Mae Johnson
Dollard des Ormeaux, Que.

Monica Matte
Montreal, Quebec

Robert McGavin
Toronto, Ontario

Linda Oliver
Halifax, Nova Scotia

Jane Pepino
Toronto, Ontario

Marie Daurice Perron
Hodgson, Manitoba

Cécile Rémillard-Beaudry
Winnipeg, Manitoba

Agnes Richard
Gander, Newfoundland

Margaret Strongitharm
Nanaimo, British Columbia

Margaret Taylor
Belleville, Ontario

Ann Tweddle
Edmonton, Alberta

Eva Voisey
Whale Cove, N.W.T.

Michelle Boivin, an assistant professor in the Civil Law Section of the University of Ottawa's Faculty of Law, specializes in company law. A founding member of the editorial board of *La Femme et le droit* and co-president of the "Women and the Law" section of the Canadian Association of Law Teachers, she has also participated in the Canadian Law Teachers' Clinics in Quebec City and Banff.

Ginette Busque, president of the Fédération des femmes du Québec, is a graduate of Laval University's law school and has worked as a volunteer with the YWCA in Montreal. A former coordinator of the Nouveau Départ program, she has also served on numerous committees and provincial task forces dealing with such topics as pension reform, pornography, and non-sexist advertising.

Julie Lee is a graduate student in the Department of Sociology, Ontario Institute for Studies in Education, Toronto. As a result of her participation in a study of the working and living conditions of southwestern Ontario farmworkers, she has become deeply concerned about the lack of awareness of these issues. Her work also focusses on an examination of societal responses to family violence, in particular, a critique of social policy responses to the sexual abuse of children.

Diane Morissette is a researcher with the Canadian Advisory Council on the Status of Women (CACSW) where her work focusses on social issues affecting Canadian women. As a social anthropologist, she has conducted field studies and published works on the participation of women in economic development and on social organization in native communities, alpine agricultural societies in Switzerland, and industrial environments in Montreal.

Pamela Smith, a sociologist at the Sample Survey and Data Bank Unit of the University of Regina, Saskatchewan, has presented numerous papers and published articles on a variety of topics, including Canada's food policy, economic trends in Canadian agriculture on the Prairies, women's contribution to agriculture in Saskatchewan, and the need for child-care services in that province.